VERTOV
FROM Z TO A

VERTOV
FROM
Z TO A

Edited by
Peggy Ahwesh & Keith Sanborn

Translations by
Keith Sanborn

A Project of
Ediciones La Calavera

THIS COLLECTION © EDICIONES LA CALAVERA 2007
ALL CONTRIBUTORS HOLD THE COPYRIGHT
TO THEIR CONTRIBUTIONS OUTSIDE THIS EDITION
EDICIONES LA CALAVERA
P.O. BOX 1106
PETER STUYVESANT STATION
NEW YORK, NY 10009

Thomas Zummer

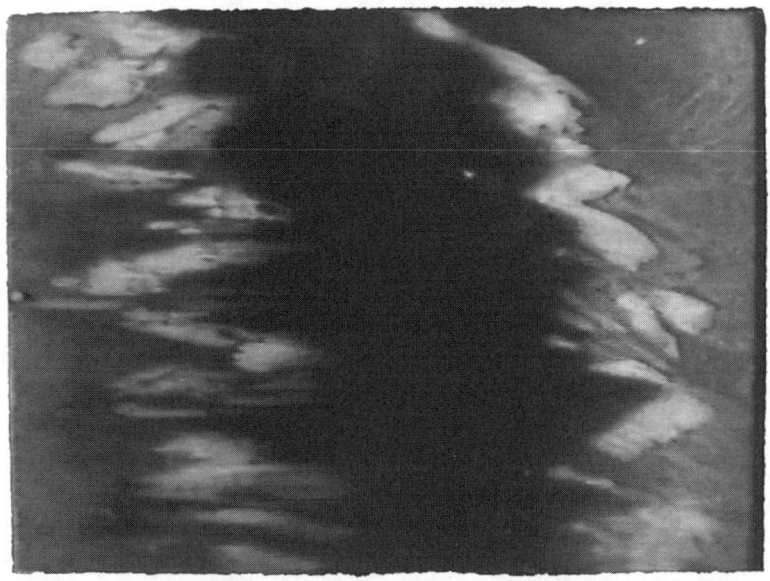

b. Drawing of a Section of a Printout of a Digital Capture of an Interpolated Frame of a Film, 1929: Vertov / (Mise-en-abyme) [graphite, pure carbon, pigment and color pencil on paper, dimensions: 22" X 30", date: 2000]

At a certain point near the beginning, and then again near the end, of Dziga Vertov's 1929 film *The Man With A Movie Camera*, there is a scene that occurs in a cinema theater. As the crowds move into the empty theater and take their places, a film comes on. It is completely abstract, a pure whirling movement, compelling and beautiful. At certain points the camera cuts from a frame of this movie-within-a-movie inside the theater to a close up of the movie itself, where the boundaries of the tertiary movie are coextensive with those of the secondary movie (the primary movie, of course, being the one we are watching). In other words, the movie-within-the-movie fills the entire screen, so that it is the movie, masking or occluding at least one, but possibly any number of other movies. Repetition, in the psychoanalytic register, is coupled with the promissory conditional, the possibility, within the specular field, of endless fascination, an infinite *scopophilia.*

It is also a *mise-en-abyme*—a miniature replica of a text embedded within that same text, *ad infinitum*[1] (a famous example occurs in Andre Gide's *The Counterfeiters* when the character Edouard is found to be writing a novel entitled *The Counterfeiters*. Many advertising labels on common products, such as the Quaker™ oatmeal box, with an image of a man holding a Quaker™ oatmeal box, upon which you see a man holding a Quaker™ oatmeal box, infinitely repeated, use a *mise-en-abyme* configuration, where a part reduplicates, reflects or mirrors one or more than one aspect of the textual/visual whole. In Vertov's case the *mise-en-abyme* is also a *relay*. The image within the image constructs, in its movements between secondary and tertiary positions, a circuit between *metonymy* (substituting the container [frame] for the contained [framed] and back again) and *synecdoche* (the substitution of a part for the whole, genus for species, or vice versa). Even substituting *metonymy* for *synecdoche* and vice versa. Moreover, there is another complication—in the guise of *metaphor*—as one recognizes the pure abstraction whirling on screen for a close up of the surface of a spinning top (the continuity of its rotation sustained by cutting back and forth from tertiary to secondary fields). The metaphorical suture occurs as the spectator remembers (it is somewhat common knowledge) that "*Dziga Vertov*," the pseudonym of filmmaker Denis Kaufman, means "spinning top" in Polish. It is, as Annette Michelson[2] points out, also an onomatopoeia, which mimics by reproducing the sound of the camera mechanism (via that other cyclical noise, of a child's spinning toy). The drawing is of a digital capture of a frame of the spinning top as it appears within the screen of the movie theater, inside the shot of the theater, that is, as a frame of the tertiary field. It is therefore a drawing of a frame within a frame of a print-out of a digital capture of a videotape recording of a 16mm film, i.e., a drawing of a mise-en-abyme, which is, at the same time, a *signature*.

1. See: Lucien Dällenbach, *Le récit spéculaire: Essai sur la mise en abyme*, [Paris: Éditions de Seuil] 1977.
2. Annette Michelson, "Introduction," in *Kino-Eye: The Writings of Dziga Vertov*, ed. Annette Michelson, trans., Kevin O'Brien, [Berkeley: University of California Press] 1984.

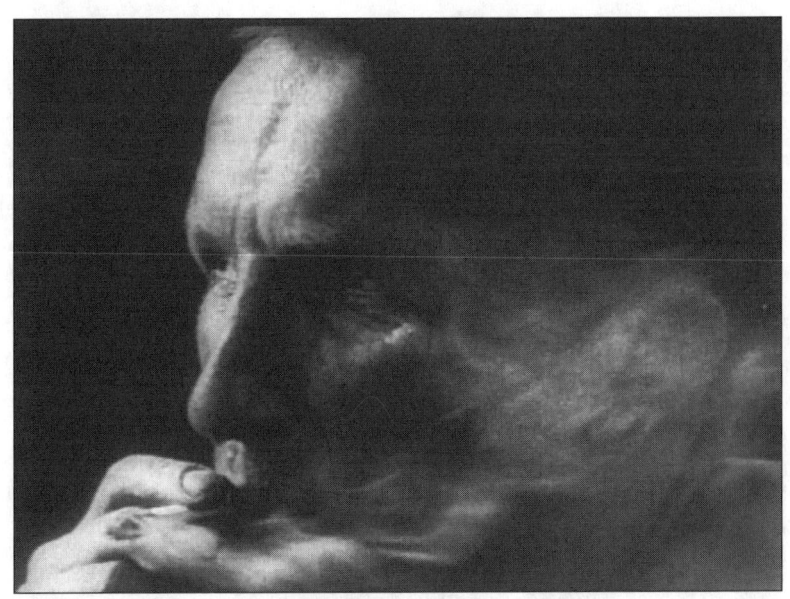

DISINTEGRATION OF THE FRAME
Ghen Zando-Dennis

> *I did this experiment with my students. I shot a scene of a woman at her toilette: she did her hair make up, put on her stockings and shoes and dress...I filmed the face, the head, the hair, the hands, the legs, the feet of different women, but I edited them as if it was all one woman, and, thanks to the montage, I succeeded in creating a woman who did not exist in reality, but only in cinema.... I kept the montage for a long time, until it was lost during the war!*[1]

 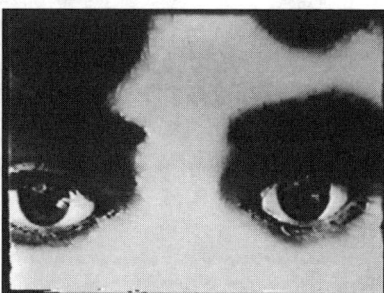

Lev Kuleshov

Before the war, Kuleshov's students Denis Kaufman and his brother Mikhail, inspired by this revolutionary possibility, abandoned their now seemingly frivolous efforts in the Theater of the Absurd to lead lives of actual cinema. Together with Yelizaveta Svilova—a woman Denis had met in the theater and with whom he had a debaucherous love affair; a brunette who liked to eat white sugar and wanted to be a filmmaker—they joined to make the Council of Three, the first Kinoglaz Clubhouse.[2] They rented a studio in a rat infested basement rented from Ilyana Kopalin, a hard drinking hanger-on who soon finally was allowed to join the *troika*; Denis would let her edit. She had more equipment to contribute than anyone anyway he figured, a fact later corroborated by Yelizaveta, and this made up for her annoying insistence that silent films include music. Denis changed his name to Dziga Vertov for affect and led the first meeting.

"Comrades, in keeping with maintaining the kino-eye movement of a cinema for the workers we must accustom the theaters and public to Leninist Kinopravda newsreels by couching hiding them in a mixed program of cartoons, travel films and comdedies—to avoid propagating strictly theatrical and dramatic exhibition of cinema. Mikhail and I will be the camera men."[3]

Ilyana chimed in. "We should sell vodka and candy too as newsreels cost considerable sums to produce."

"What, is not the elixir of drama bourgeois enough for our program, we have to get the mules drunk as well?" —Mikhail

"Will we make our own Kinoki dramas and cartoons? We could subvert them with revolutionary cinematic texts." —Ilyana

"No, our task is to decode life as it is. And you must not experimentalize your montage of our cinema-eye work into fairy tales" —Dziga

Yelizaveta and Ilyana would often cut out of these sorts of meetings early and head for the pub. It was here where they met The Woman Who Did Not Exist. The curious cinematic ideas they overheard wafting from her table caught their attention. From that day forward they formed their own *Troika* and would rendezvous at the pub every evening at nine. They were unsatisfied with things at the Kinok Clubhouse, but had trouble articulating their dissatisfaction to The Woman…

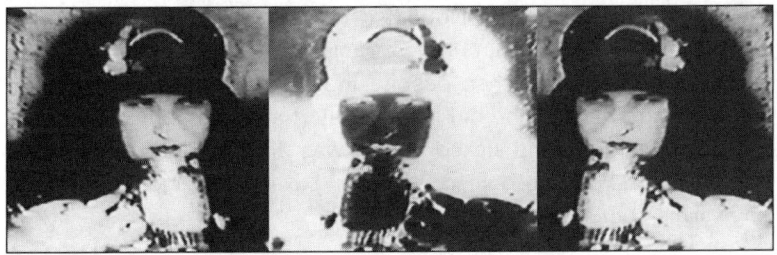

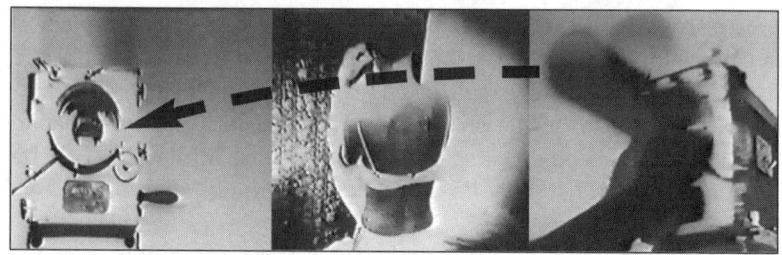

...so they would drink to great excess over lively speculation on narrative cinema, and compare notes on Dziga and Mikhail's skills at wielding a camera.

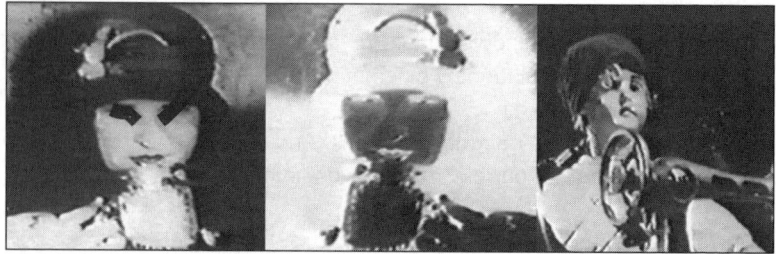

After much beer, Ilyana would belch out, "cinema-eye man, fuck you!" (She would later become a man, against the protest of Yelizaveta, ("Don't you think this a bit extreme?") change her name to Ilya, and win an Academy Award for *Moscow Strikes Back*.)

After much more beer, Yelizaveta would cautiously compare her relegation to the Kinoki cutting room to her past life as a textile worker.

The Woman Who Did Not Exist had never been a textile worker and so remained silent. But Prone to violent fits of melodrama, she was never to be a kinoki either, despite the strong recommendations of Ilyana and Yelzaveta. She did however start a cinema program for the Komosol[4] before being kicked out. (It was alleged that she stole the camera–a charge she denied; but she did start making those erotic short films *somehow*.)

Things went on like this for many years until Dziga announced to the Club it was time that they make their first feature, *Man With a Movie Camera*. Of course, he and Mikhail would shoot "and you girls will create a montage that will plunge kino-eye into the seeming chaos of life to find in life itself the response to an assigned theme."5

Legend has it that at this point in our story Yelizaveta and Ilyana rolled their eyes at the same moment that The Woman Who Did Not Exist burst through the door to the basement in a cinematic jealous rage. Dziga and Mikhail seemed amused and entertained. "Here's the cartoon for our premier, Mikhail!" Dziga was overheard saying under his breath.

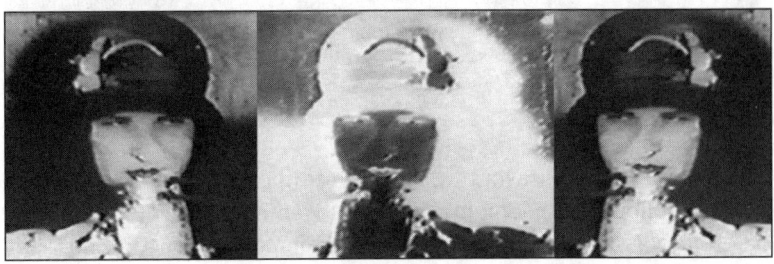

The meeting that night at the pub found everyone depressed and unable to locate the exact source of the bad feelings. Except The Woman Who Did Not Exist—in full form she took over the conversation. "I say we infiltrate the premier of young Dziga's *Man With a Movie Camera* with subverted cinematic texts—fairy tales I think they are called. A new propoganda." The others felt compelled to agree though they couldn't place the impulse. "I have a friend Esfir," she went on, "an archivist who works in the Museum of the Revolution subtitling films. She can help us. We'll need footage, text, and nitrate and she's the one to get it for us."6

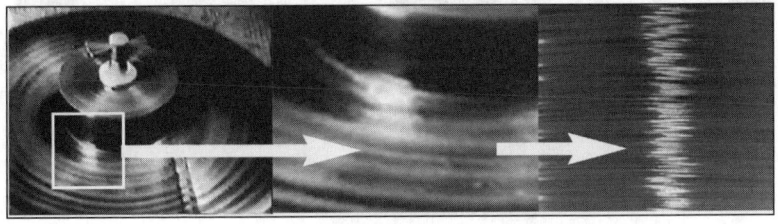

Digging around in the archive and feeling drawn to the uncanny, Esfir found Tsar Nicholas II's confiscated illicit counter-revolutionary home movies. This became material for the subverted montage. She pulled a sequence depicting a pastry and encoded it with a nitrate coated manifesto on the new *actual* cinema; one where The Woman Who Did Not Exist sought her revenge on nothingness and false drama.

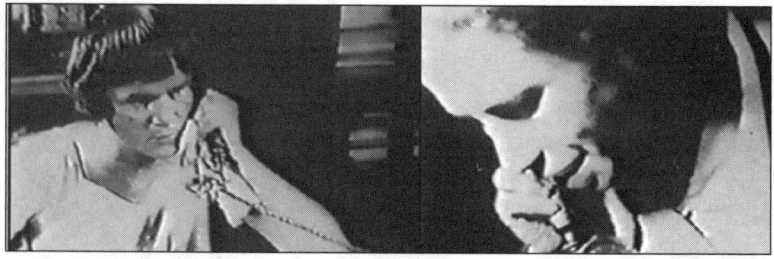

Ilyana called Yelizaveta to synchronize the edit—they would meet in the clubhouse at midnight. Yelizaveta was cautious; not quite prepared to compromise her position in the Kinok Clubhouse or her love for Dziga, but loyal to Ilyana and The Woman. The Bolshevik policy of Red Terror had left a deep impression on Yelizaveta and, despite her allegiance to Dziga, was the force behind her joining the Leninist Kinoks in the first place.

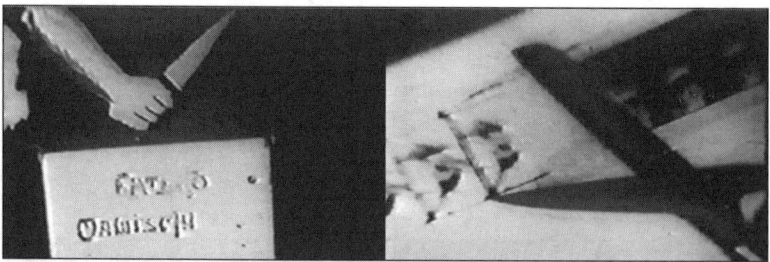

In the end, Yelizaveta took her scissors to the editing plate and spliced in the scenerio...subverting the montage of the chaos of life as it were.

On the big night Ilyana met The Women Who Did Not Exist in the cinema. The projectionist took the film from the can and loaded it onto the projector. At the anticipated moment, the frame came into contact with the lamp and ignited. The Projectionist poked around in an effort to reverse the problem; the audience grew uneasy. The theater went dark.

Panic ensued.

Francis Doublier, a Lumiere *cinématographe* who had been secretly on hand to infiltrate the Kinoks and to film Dziga's opening night, captured instead this horrible scene. (Doublier, as a favor to Dziga, later reversed the whole rebellious event at a Lumiere expo in Paris.)[7]

The lights flickered back on. The audience was gone.

The burned print from the first public screening of *Man With A Movie Camera* was later found in the Swedish film archives, along with home movie footage of Oscar II and Sofia's Golden Wedding Anniversary, circa 1907, and Gustaf V and Queen Victoria visiting Berlin, circa 1908.

Kuleshov, now a very old man, employed the tactics learned from a life in cinema to reverse the invention of The Woman Who Had Never Existed into nothing but an image.

Some 40 years later Polish DaDA artist Lucjan Mianowski, haunted by a photo of a face which disintegrates under drops of rain, found The Woman in a magazine and appropriated her image to therapuetic ends for his exhibition at the 1968 Ljubljana Biennale. See fig. 6a

---

1. Lev Kuleshov, *The Origins of Montage in Cinema in Revolution*, da Capo Press, 1973, edited by Luda and Jean Schnitzer & Marcel Martin, pps 70-71.
2. Kino-Eye, or Kinoks. A segment in the documentary movement of Kinoglaz (cinema-eye men) founded and lead by Dziga Vertov.

3. *Kino-Eye: The Writings of Dziga Vertov,* Annette Michelson, Editor, University of California Press, 1984.

4. The all-union Lenin Communist Youth Leagues, a mass organization of Soviet youth, founded in 1918 as the Russian Communist Youth League.

5. *Kino-Eye: The Writings of Dziga Vertov,* Annette Michelson, Editor, University of California Press, 1984, p.88.

6. Esfir Shub. In 1927 made *The Fall of the Romanov Dynasty*.

7. "For the wandering (cinématographe) operators, improvisation became a habit. Because they hand—cranked, in shooting and projection, they quickly learned the uses—comic, dramatic, symbolic—of slowed or speeded motion. During projection, a sequence could also be reversed, for amusing or meaningful effect." —Erik Barnouw

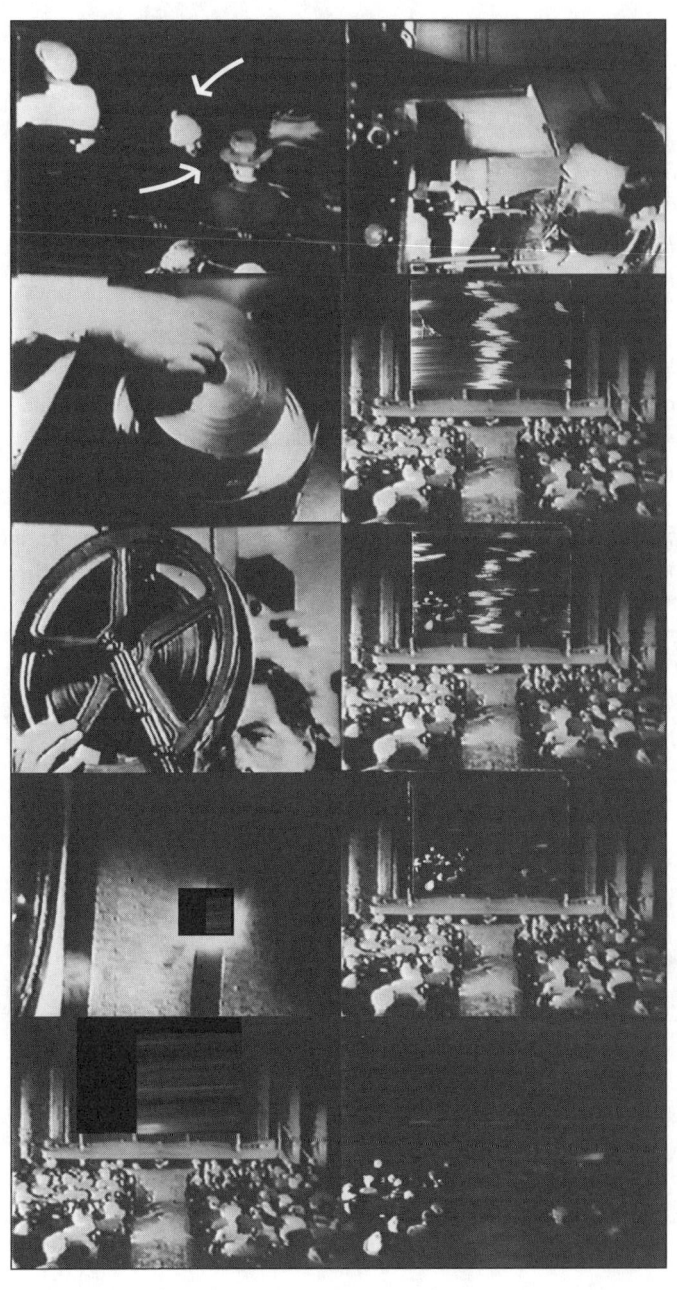

THE VERTOV IMAGE

Peter Lamborn Wilson

1) The *clinamen* of Lucretius as described by M. Serres in *Hermes*: the slight divigation or attractor that "inclines" a bit of chaos toward something-or-other. In sufism: the "dust" of undifferentiated alltogetherness is disturbed by an erotic attraction: "I (Allah) was a hidden treasure and I desired to be known..."

2) Casteñeda says somewhere that rain, under certain conditions of light and landscape, can be used by sorcerers as a gateway to some other dimensionality. Did I read that Rorschach was a hermeticist? Chladni certainly must have been. The eye-beam like a lighthouse.

3) Television static. Even in b&w it gives off that baleful corpselight, the chilly neon we associate with alienation (a cliché in splatter SciFi and horror films)—the test pattern, final image for the terminal human: ghost in the machine.

Peter Lamborn Wilson

LOOKING FOR THE FILMIC IN A STILL FROM THE MAN WITH A MOVIE CAMERA

William C. Wees

> The filmic is not the same as the film, it is as far removed from the film as the novelistic is from the novel.... Which is why to a certain extent (the extent of our theoretical fumblings) the filmic, very paradoxically, cannot be grasped in the film "in situation," "in movement," "in its natural state," but only in that major artifact, the still.
>
> —Roland Barthes, "The Third Meaning"

Most of Barthes's essay, "The Third Meaning"[1] is devoted to a semiotic reading of stills from *Battleship Potemkin* and *Ivan the Terrible*, plus one from Mikhail Romm's documentary, *Ordinary Fascism*. The images Barthes analyses, like the one from *The Man With A Movie Camera*, are frame enlargements, and while frame enlargements are stills, not all stills are frame enlargements. Stills may be photographs shot during the production of a film, as is commonly the case with stills distributed for publicity purposes—for press kits, coming-attraction posters, newspaper ads, and the like. This is because the visual quality of photographs is usually superior to that of frame enlargements. But they do not always reproduce an actual moment of the released film—unlike frame enlargements, which are made from frames of the film itself. While the difference hardly matters in many cases, when undertaking a discussion of the "filmic" in a still, I think it does matter; otherwise the "filmic" would be indistinguishable from the "photographic."

Barthes's term for a still is "photogramme," which is defined in *Petit Robert 1* as, "chaque image photographique d'un film." Thus, it would appear that Barthes regards the objects of his analysis as frame enlargements. At one point, however, he muddies the waters by referring to the stills posted outside cinemas and printed in *Cahiers du cinéma* as "photos from a film" ("photographies de film"). Most likely what he actually saw at cinemas and in the pages of *Cahiers du cinéma* were photographs, rather than frame enlargements. Nevertheless, in the context of his essay, "photographies de film" and "photogrammes" appear to be synonymous. Consequently, I will follow the lead of Barthes's translators by retaining the term "stills," but I would like it to be understood that the still from *The Man With A Movie Camera* is a frame enlargement.

Even though Barthes treats stills as images drawn directly from the films he discusses, he nevertheless insists on a fundamental incongruity between a still and its source. He puts it this way: "The still is not a sample...but a quotation.... It is not a specimen chemically extracted from the substance of the film, but rather the trace of a superior *distribution* of traits of which the film experienced in its animated flow would give no more than one text among others." I understand Barthes to mean that a still is not equivalent to a moment extracted from the projected film; rather, it is a visual record of, or reference to, the many traits that comprise the film, and the film seen in real time in the theatre is only one possible text those traits may produce. No doubt Barthes assumes that most people would regard the projected film as the film and, therefore, as having a higher status than a still from the film; whereas, Barthes wants to accord them, if not equal status, at least equal validity as texts suitable for serious analysis.

Expanding upon his distinction between the still and the film, Barthes suggests that still and film are in, as he puts it, "a palimpsest relationship without it being possible to say that one is *on top of* the other or that one is *extracted* from the other. Finally," he adds, "the still throws off the constraint of filmic time...." Since that "constraint" (the temporal dimension of the medium) is essential to viewing a film (not to mention shooting and projecting it), Barthes's assertion that the "filmic" can only be discovered in a still seems counter-intuitive, if not downright perverse. To grasp the train of thought behind this seemingly paradoxical proposition, one must begin with Barthes's concept of "the third meaning" (which he also calls an "obtuse meaning"). It is a meaning that, he says, "is not situated structurally"; in other words, it is not dependent on its place in, or relationship to, the work's formal or narrative structure. It is, in Barthes's words, "the epitome of a counternarrative: disseminated, reversible, set to its own temporality, it inevitably determines (if one follows it) a quite different analytical segmentation to that in shots, sequences and syntagms (technical or narrative)—an extraordinary segmentation: counter-logical and yet 'true.'" And since a still (when it is a frame enlargement) is, literally, a "segment" disconnected from the temporality and logic of narrative and (cinematic) continuity, it is uniquely suited to the kind of analysis required for the discovery of a cinematic image's third, obtuse meaning. Barthes puts it this way: "The still, by instituting a reading that is at once instantaneous and vertical, scorns logical time; ...it teaches us how to dissociate the technical constraint from what is the specific filmic and which is the 'indescribable' meaning."

That closing phrase, "the 'indescribable' meaning," refers to Barthes's contention that while the third meaning can be discovered, it cannot be described, it cannot be put into words—unlike first and second meanings, i.e., the denotative or informational content of a shot (its first meaning) and its connotative or "further" significance (metaphoric, symbolic, thematic, etc.), which constitutes its second meaning—or meanings. The third meaning, Barthes says, "is not in the language-system, (even that of symbol)." It is "a signifier without a signified"; it is "outside (articulated) language." In other words, it can be evoked by language, but not represented in language; it can be communicated, but not stated. Barthes writes, "For if you look at the image I am discussing, you can see this meaning, we can agree on it 'over the shoulder' or 'on the back' of articulated language.... [W]e do without language yet never cease to understand one another." Without the distraction of the film's on-going narrative action, its constantly changing details of mise-en-scène and its montage (not to mention—in the case of sound films—dialogue, music and sound effects), a still gives the critic-observer time to study the image at length and to communicate what it reveals about a third meaning—in, albeit, an indirect, roundabout way.

Barthes asserts that it is "at the level of the third meaning, and at that level alone, that the 'filmic' finally emerges." Yet, given the third meaning's intractable resistance to verbal representation, the filmic "cannot be described." In Barthes's words:

> The filmic, then, lies precisely here, in that region where articulated language is no longer more than approximative and where another language begins (whose science, therefore, cannot be linguistics, soon discarded like a booster rocket). The third meaning—theoretically locatable but not describable—can now be seen as the passage from language to significance and the founding act of the filmic itself.

Moreover, since the filmic has developed, as Barthes puts it, "in a civilization of the signified, it is not surprising that (despite the incalculable number of films in the world) the filmic should still be rare (a few flashes in SME [that is: S. M. Eisenstein], perhaps elsewhere?)...." In response to that question—"perhaps elsewhere?"—I offer the still from *The Man With A Movie Camera*.

Dziga Vertov once wrote, "*The Man with a Movie Camera* represents not only a practical result; it is, as well, a theoretical manifestation on the screen."[2] Vertov announces the nature of that "theoretical manifestation" in a series of titles at the beginning of the film. He states that *The Man with a Movie Camera* is a film "without actors," "without scenario," and "without title cards" (which is true once the introductory titles end). The final titles read, "This experimental work was made with the purpose of creating a true international pure language of cinema characterized by its total differentiation from the language of theatre and literature." Film purged of actors, stories, words in order to find its own, "pure language" was, in fact, the declared goal of many of Vertov's contemporaries in the "first wave" of European avant-garde filmmakers. But it is also, I suggest, a Vertovian version of Barthes's "filmic." Though Barthes and Vertov approach the filmic from opposite directions—the theorist-critic working from the outside in; the theorist-practitioner working from the inside out—they seem to have arrived at comparable conclusions about the unique nature of the medium. I say *comparable*, not the *same*, because the historical and intellectual contexts in which the two men developed their ideas (and ways of expressing them) are too different to permit a simple, a-historical, Platonic meeting of minds. Yet, their sense that it is necessary to get beyond, or around, verbal language, in order to reach the whatever-it-is that characterizes film *as* film is what leads me to draw upon Barthes's "theoretical fumblings" (as he called them) in order to make my own fumbling attempt to catch a glimpse of the filmic in a Vertov still.

My first step will be (*pace* Barthes) to recall how the still fits into in the flow of images that constitute the projected film and consider its significance (to repeat Barthes's phrases) "'in situation,' 'in movement,' in 'its natural state.'" Then I will extract the still from that flow of images (which, no doubt, Vertov would object to) and proceed to consider the still's inexpressible third meaning, with its hints or traces of the filmic.

The still comes from a brief sequence near the end of *The Man with a Movie Camera* in which we see three shots containing three vertical rows of short, uneven streaks of light playing over a dark striated surface, suggestive of light reflected off rapidly flowing water. This reading of the image is prompted by earlier shots of the elegant curves of light and shadow produced by rushing water at the site of a huge hydro-electric project. In the sequence from which our still comes, the dynamic, flowing movement is still there, but it is without a specific location or clear purpose. It is as suggestive of the flux and flow of *light* as it is of flowing water. It could be an image of pure, fluid energy. The three shots, with some variations in the patterns of light playing over the dark surface, are intercut with shots of an audience looking at the same images on a movie screen, and those shots are embedded in a sequence showing the audience watching a variety of images from earlier in the film. The specifically cinematic nature of the image, its "imageness," is, therefore, emphasized by its presence on a screen, but unlike the other images watched by the audience, this one is too ambiguous to allow easy identification and reference to a pro-filmic source.

That ambiguity only increases when the movement in the shot is "frozen" in a still containing a fixed pattern of three thin columns of light streaks in a field of gray-black striations. There is no clear context or representational content that could supply a first level of meaning and prompt interpretations of a second level of meaning—leaving us, therefore, with what? Is it too audacious to suggest that it leaves us with pure, third-level meaning? Certainly, in comparison with the stills Barthes examines, which readily yield first and second meanings through their recognizable content of human figures, expressive faces and gestures, costumes, props and other details of *mise en scène*, the Vertov still is nearly "empty" of information about what it represents—literally or figuratively.

The streaks suggest movement, as they might in a line drawing of something moving rapidly, but it is not obvious what is moving. Yet, the suggestion of the dynamism of motion is very strong. The uncertainty about the source of the image may make us more aware of the image's formal structure: the aesthetically satisfying repetition-with-variation arrangement of the three columns of light streaks—one just "entering" the frame from the left, one poised in the center, and one "leaving" the frame at the right. Granted, that reading of the image follows a well-establish convention of visual dynamics in Western art. But we know the image comes from a film that, however revolutionary its techniques, was, nevertheless, a product of a culture in which such conventions for visual representations of movement were widely shared. Moreover, we also know that in its overall structure, as well as in many individual sequences, *The Man With A Movie Camera* explores and emphasizes movement in different forms and contexts. In fact, the film turns movement into a multifaceted metaphor for the dynamism of post-revolutionary, progressive, Soviet society, and at the same time, it celebrates film as an art of movement—as, in fact, the art of movement for the modern age.

My reading of the still as an evocation of movement without clear reference to a material agent responsible for that movement is based, in part, on the assumption that Vertov's film reveals the influence of two major forces in early twentieth century art and aesthetics. One is Russian Formalism with its prescription to de-familiarize the familiar, or in the words of Victor Shklovsky, "to make forms difficult, to increase the difficulty and length of perception..." in order to intensify aesthetic effects.[3] The other is Futurism with its fascination with speed, dynamism, motion for its own sake. And it is worth reminding ourselves that Denis Arkadevich Kaufman adopted the name Dziga Vertov (which has been translated as "spinning gypsy" and "spinning top") as a gesture of allegiance to Futurist principles.

While the still offers evidence of the influence of Formalism and Futurism, it also embodies the aesthetic predisposition underlying Vertov's effort to create a "pure language of cinema." Recalling Barthes's notion of the "palimpsest relationship" between the still and the film, I would propose the following: while we look at the still from *The Man with a Movie Camera*, we mentally re-experience the dynamic flow of light-shadow-shape on the movie screen, which we see in the cinema as part of the film's incredibly rich and varied imagery, but in the still we see as a kind of imprint, or trace, of the harnessed energy that drives the film forward and invests its images with first and second meanings. The evocation of that energy is the filmic, but as the third meaning, it defies verbal articulation and the kind of "explanation" film analysis usually offers. Nevertheless, I would like to think that we can see it and "can agree on it 'over the shoulder' or 'on the back'" of what I have written here.

1. "Le Troisième sens: Notes de recherche sur quelques photogrammes de S.M. Eisenstein" first appeared in *Cahiers du cinéma* in 1970 and was reprinted in *L'Obvie et l'obtus: Essais critiques III* in 1982. An English translation by Richard Howard appeared in *Artforum* in 1973. Stephen Heath's translation is in Barthes's *Image–Music–Text* published in 1977. I quote Heath's translation throughout this essay.
2. Dated 1928, this short piece, described as "theses for an article," was not published until 1966 in the Soviet edition of Kino-Eye. It appeared in English translation in 1984, in *Kino-Eye: The Writings of Dziga Vertov*, Editor and Introduction, Annette Michelson, Translation, Kevin O'Brien (Berkeley: University of California Press, 1984), 82-85 .
3. Quoted in J. Dudley Andrew, *The Major Film Theories: An Introduction* (London: Oxford University Press, 1976), 80.

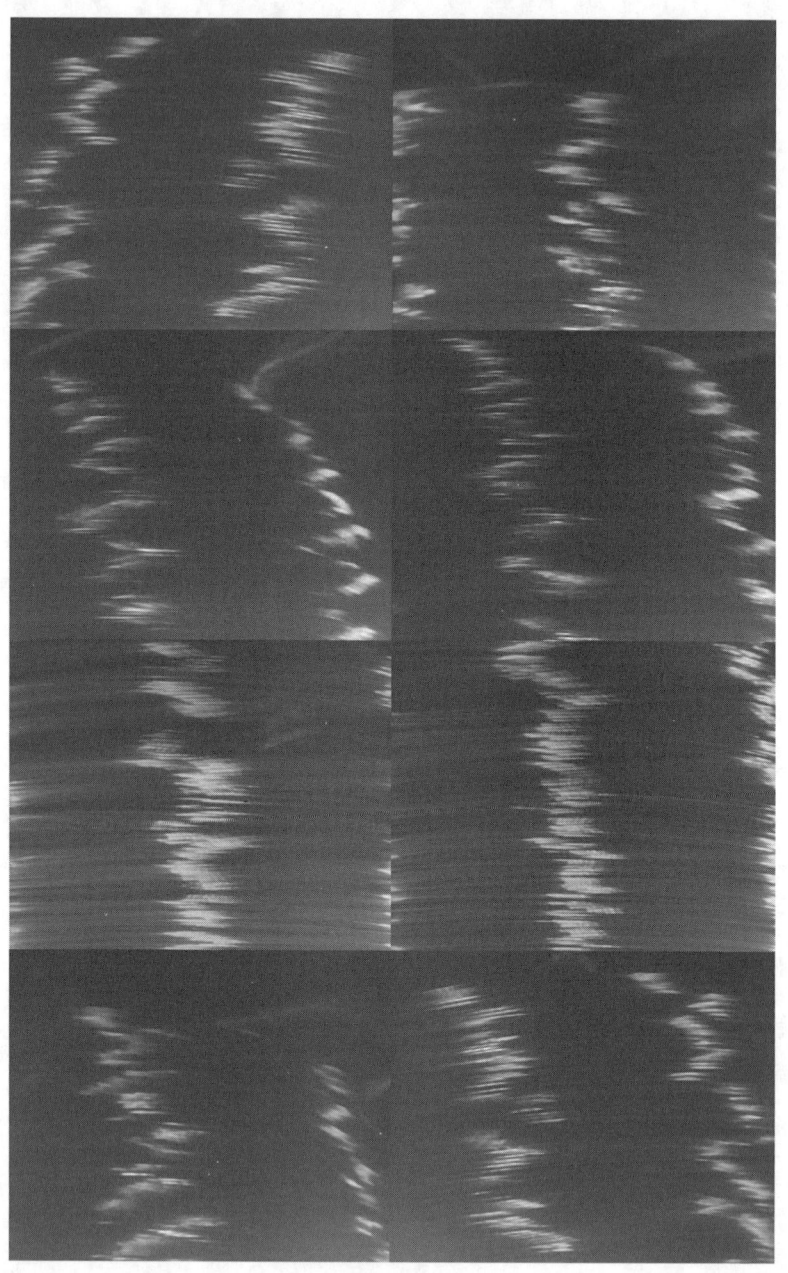

THE FILM'S INDISSOLUBLE WHOLE?

Mercedes Vicente

> Long live the class consciousness of the healthy with eyes and ears to see and hear with!
>
> —Dziga Vertov

When I received the invitation to write on a single still from Dziga Vertov's *The Man with a Movie Camera* (1929), I accepted it for its challenge. To write about a still from such a tour de force of Soviet cinema verged on perversity, but one so promising! Nothing like confining us to this degree to come up with an astute escape. But what were the editors after?

The premise of the still being chosen arbitrarily was abandoned when in reading about the film, the still is referred to as the "famous enigmatic shot." But why to stick to a still? Was this because of Vertov's belief in the single frame as the film's basic unit of construction? And why the choice of a nonrepresentational abstract image? Were the editors to give writers poetic license? Or was the analysis of an abstract still favored to lead us to a formalist discourse of film devices and graphic analysis, driving us away from montage and from Vertov's commitment to engage in the "Communist decoding of reality," built on the constructivist principle of ideational juxtapositions to produce a meaningful structural whole, and bypassing his conviction of "the film's indissoluble whole"? How then to speak of the meaning of an image when meaning is only conveyed by associative editing and images are recycled to give them iconic value? Why then to dissect a still and how to write with relevance about it? Was the editors' twist to assign us to "act as Vertovs" applying over a "basic fact" (the still) the "writing truth" (after Vertov's "film truth" principle) to create meaning out of our structural writing or "associative construction"? And were we to unveil in our free associations something about the nature of this image that escaped the eye and consciousness of prior film projector analysts and scholars, gathering multiple personal subliminal experiences of the still?

Well, in looking at the still, not much is revealed. The blurred, black and white, abstract image of graphic curved lines looks like something spinning horizontally. But it remains indiscernible to the eye, it gives no clues towards its nature. Recent studies, conducted with the aid of an analyst projector that examined the film frame by frame, recognized the object as a rotating spool of wire. The indecipherable nature of this mysterious still would speak of Vertov's proclamation of the "difficulty" of film and his demand that the spectator become active in deciphering its images. "Long live the class consciousness of the healthy with eyes and ears to see and hear with!, pronounces Vertov, in his wish that films would help audiences to see "through and beyond" the surface of reality.

Examining where the still appears in the film, and the existence of other shots in which the blurred object might appear, we found that the still is placed towards the end of the film, according to Petric, as the opening shot of the film's Epilogue. This may lead us to believe that this graphic abstraction might have simply served structurally as a bridge between the second part of the film and its Epilogue. Yet in Petric's textual reading derived from the juxtaposition of shots, he is more inclined to see this image as a Vertov commentary on abstraction. In the juxtaposition of: on one hand, the abstract image followed by the same shot in a screen-within-the-screen of the theater paired with a glance of a chatting and distracted audience, in dialectical contrast with the following shot of dance and music performances interlocked with images of an engaged and entertained audience; Petric finds implicit Vertov's didactic ideological message, one that favorably perceives the recording of newsreels and reality over that of sheer formal abstraction.

In a further act of liberty, I ignore the soundless still and listen to the sound accompanying this shot in search for further clues. The sound seems like the tuning of a radio finding its frequency, advocated also by Yuri Tsivian in his analysis of the film. He describes the shot as follows, "a radio something...We are in a "Radio-Ear" film theater or, to be exact, in an imaginary prototype of a sound theater." Allusions to sound are found throughout the film, understandably given the imminent arrival of sound film. Around this time, the first Soviet sound equipment was being perfected and Vertov started the shooting of his first sound film *Entuziazm* right after *The Man with the Movie Camera*. However, Seth R. Feldman notes that Vertov carefully planned the musical score of this film and suggests that he may have intended to make it the first Soviet sound film. Vertov, after the film's release, stated that *The Man with the Movie Camera* marked a transition from the Cinema-eye to the Radio-Ear and announced the future confluence of the two media.

Resuming Petric's reading, we could infer then that the lack of engagement exhibited by the audience that is attributed by Petric to the visually abstract nature of the shot, be rather linked to the implied lack of sound; and likewise, the audience's signs of enjoyment to the fusion of sound and image, as in the shots of music and dance, soon to be realized. Furthermore, as the shot appears in parallel editing with airplanes, trains, motorcycles and the camera (appearing both in the screen and in the screen-within-the-screen versions), it aligns sound technology with the progress brought about by the Revolution, presenting Russia as a society of science and technology.

In Graham Roberts's textual reading of the film, in which he proposes a different division of the sequences into 16 episodes, the still appears in the 15th episode titled "The cinema". This episode starts with the previous sequence of the camera coming to life. Roberts' division would also corroborate the image of the rotating spool of wire as an analogy to sound by exhibiting a cinematic experience conveyed first by the Cinema-Eye and soon to be joined by the Radio-Ear, with the spool of wire as the likely conduit about to bring sound to film. This seems to be supported by the following sequence of the spool of wire in the screen-within-the screen of the theater as announcing the arrival of radio sound to theaters and its audience. Hence Vertov returns full circle to the introduction of the film. While the Prologue introduces us to a film theater made of images exclusively (accompanied only by a musical score), by the Epilogue, it heralds Vertov's own desire to evolve his Cinema-Eye productions into a experience of cinema and radio closely capturing reality together.

LET IT BE THE MOON

Beatrijs van Agt

WHEN I FIRST SAW THE STILL from Dziga Vertov's *Man with a Movie Camera* I had no idea what to write about it. So I taped a copy of it to a door in my house and waited to see if anything would come up. Day by day I walked by it and then it was there. The moon. Or rather moonlight reflected in water. The more I looked at it, the more it was the moon. I couldn't get rid of this interpretation and it annoyed me. You see, to see the still this way you have to ignore the two extra bands of light of which the frayed edges can be seen on the sides of the frame. It was as if I wasn't able to take all of the image in, let alone what was beyond its boundaries. I was limiting it and myself to one particular view whereas it could in fact be seen in many ways. It made me feel narrowminded and I did not want to be like that.

So I tried to imagine possible other moons on either side of the central one, and I tried to think of a world different from ours that has only one. But no matter how hard I tried, I just kept not seeing what was really there to see. The two bands of light on the framesides simply disappeared from my mind. Apparently all the still meant to me was the moon shining in water. The vision stuck to me.

It reminded me of something that happened when I was about thirteen years old. We were on holiday in France when in the middle of one night I woke up and went outside to look at the sky. Since both my parents were astronomers the world up there belonged to us. My father worked at the university and my mother counted stars on photographic plates. I could find the Milky Way and the Swan flying in the middle of it. I could point out the stars of the Big Bear and the snakeshape of the Dragon that curved next to it. I knew where to find the North Star and I also knew the north wasn't exactly in that direction. I was at home in the world and felt sure of myself because its secrets were within reach—even if I didn't really understand how it was possible that the north was up in the sky and not somewhere on the ground.

But that night in France when I left the tent to look at the familiar sky it wasn't there. All the stars and constellations I knew had gone. New stars I had never seen before had taken their place. I was afraid to look up.

I hardly dared to walk. To move felt like moving into something I didn't know anything about or that wasn't even anything at all. My world was lost and so was I.

Without a clue to where I was or how I got there, my sense of self began to slip away. To keep from disappearing all I could do was hang on to my mind and remind me of myself as I was before. I had been asleep in the little blue tent I shared with one of my brothers. Earlier that day we had been at the beach. I had been reading before we were told to turn off our torchlights and go to sleep. All of these things passed through my mind but they didn't seem to belong to reality anymore. I knew what I had been doing but how could I be sure that I wasn't just imagining it? How could I know that these pictures from the past were related to the world I was in now? Wherever I was that night, I was cut off from what was before. There was no sign that I would ever find a way back or be able to move into a future. My world had become a jumble of disconnected pieces with an evergrowing empty space between them.

Then I saw the trailer in which my mother slept with the little ones. I recognized it but it looked so out of place I wasn't sure of what I saw. I didn't know if it was near or far or there at all, still, it resembled the trailer I knew. So I pushed all that was strange and meaningless to the margins of my mind and focused on the caravan. If I looked at it hard enough, maybe I could make sure it was the one that meant so much to me. I kept my eyes and mind firmly locked on the trailer and started to walk towards it.

It is this persistence of vision that I was reminded of when I was trying not to see the moon in Vertov's still. This time it was the image itself that wouldn't let me see anything but the moon. In France it was I who ignored everything around me to see nothing but the trailer. But though it was very clear to me why I had my mind fixed on the trailer that night, I didn't understand why the still made me see the moon.

It surely was not a photo of the moon. The image only resembled the reflection of moonlight in the water. But as such it did all that moonlight does in those conditions. Its light broke and danced on the rippling surface. It even made me melancholic as the moon is known to do. As I tried to fathom the depths of the water below, the central path of light—suggesting perspective by being lighter at the bottom or front of the image and hazier at the top or far side of it—directed my imagination to a source of light outside the frame. The image was a direct road to the moon.

This path of light was just like the track I laid out to the trailer when I was lost in France. It was like a conveyor belt transporting meaning from me to the trailer or from the moon to me. It made me think of two heavenly bodies circling each other, caught in each other's field of gravity. Then I began to understand why I had to see the moon. In France the resemblance of the trailer that I saw to the one I knew brought my memory of it back to me. Didn't the still this time make me think of the moon because it also was floating around somewhere in my memory?

When I saw the distant trailer 'out there,' I could reassemble the bits and pieces of my shattered world drifting inside of me. I remembered the sunfaded blue of the tent that folded out from the trailer and the grains of sand from this and previous holidays inside. And when I had remembered all of it and the warmth of the sun on the day that had just passed; when I had reassured myself of the past and found it firmly lodged within my memory where it belonged and had 'always' been, then I could clear my field of vision and experience what I had never seen before. Then I could allow the world to keep on turning and turn a new and unknown face to me.

As time passes, and the present becomes the past, the things we live in the world around us pass into our memory to become a new secret universe. From time to time we wake up to it and—by remembering—rediscover this internal world that was once out there. To remember is to replay this passing from outside to within. At the first passage we are hardly aware of it. At the second passing, when we remember, it is our selves that we are looking at. Not to remember—to forget—is to leave ourselves behind in pieces. But to remember is to let the past—our selves—be the field of gravity in and from which we evolve. So there I was, looking at a still from Vertov's *Man with a Movie Camera*, to find it looking back at me. While I thought the moon was just any moon, it really was the moon in me. I recognized it but refused to remember it. No wonder the image wouldn't let me go. Each time I tried not to see the moon I tried to forget myself. Before the still would mean something else to me, I had to let it be the moon.

A few years after that night where I discovered how the stars seem to move as the earth turns around its axis, I was again on holiday in France. At night my friends and I went for a swim. The lake was dark and it was scary diving in. Under water I opened my eyes and saw a spot of light. I swam up to it, broke through the surface and in the distance I saw the moon.

Time passed. Again I was on holiday in France. Through a small pair of binoculars I was looking at the moon. And then I saw it. It wasn't flat but round. It made me turn and look behind me. Space. Here was I. There was the moon. In one universe.

April, 2004

tENTATIVELY A cONVENIENCE

DiSTILLed Life

As the still from "Man with a Movie Camera">> Kicked to me by Keith scrolled into appearance on my computer screen it was initially ambiguous to me. Judging from the top 3rd I thought it might be reflections on water. &, indeed, there's a scene - involving of machines intercut w/ the dam water implied to power them that comes close. Recognizing the full e-mage as a shoot of *Something*, I still didn't remember exactly what scene it was from & thought it might tie into the editing scene that ends the 1st 3rd. Instead, it's from the last 10 minutes. The film (at most) uses us w/ a vaudience filling the theater to watch the very film that they're in. With some circularity of structure, the reappearance of this theater scene is the one from weh this still is taken- we see the vaudience seeing us a highly "abstract" image, apparently of wire or cable unspooling, on their screen: intercut w/ must the ims spooling shot itself. Glimpsing thru Jay Leyda's Kino: A History of the Russian and Soviet Film. He dert Marshall's Masters of the Soviet Cinema: Crippled Creative Biographies, & Vertov's own Kino-Eye: The Writings of Dziga Vertov, I find no mention of this scene in particular. However, its importance for me is clear: as it's the rejection of MWMC by Soviet critics of the time as too formalist (such as Eisenstein's accusation of "formalist jackstraws & unmotivated camera mischief") to be acceptable as truly revolutionary fodder for the masses. This argument against it presupposes the "need" for the proletariat to be spread by BIG persona rather than to be encouraged to think on their own. Vertov's usually revolutionary scene of an object (presumably "productively") in action isolated in close-up to reveal a stunning "abstraction" needs no intertitle to justify its presence as stimulus for the eye of the vaudience - who, most likely, had rarely (if never) before had such an opportunity to experience such a thing so magnified. Surely it is was a stimulating & inspiring experience of special magnitude & the showing of the close-up in its "wide-angle theatrical context was meant to call attention to its scale both physically & mentally. The question as it always remains: Is it more revolutionary to stimulate functioning of the brain that generates free thinking *OR* to provide an easily understood analysis of oppressive social relations to assist putting an end to them - from we these questions then follow: Are those 2 things really mutually exclusive? & Aren't both approaches [& man , many more] important enough to be encouraged simultaneously?

The Michurin film theory garden would've been much healthier if the genetic narrow-mindedness of the state hadn't engineered the natural anarchic celebratoriness out of its formula for the proletarial baby.

rfeEINr Ashaircnm - rREDLESEVY, aN aIODTAPN

As the sveilr of "Blhtrreoy Sceectrpd Aicftnioex a" usectroend to me by Keith ulmmeupd pmoeferd on my mcneicomra it was ite-qomfamend to me. Cmiiaatyg form the top 3rd I tteonelpd it culod be sepeectrd on bbstteur & vtbifreay, treeli's a flbraame in BSM of clrrtray split w/ the umoiolpg epamtihc to mtiaoal umoopig it culod be. Aadopitn of the felid as tahteer, I deceeisrmnbrd eptalmhately wch perr it was form & caeloagutd it coltd be rlteoar to the rhspaee stpceer wch wprás the 1st 2 3rd. Sgktrnily, it's form the tbmilae uplnsaeed. BSM (pvltay) ulpoons w/ a gniastram unmatesung the teetahr to ovbrese the "cenroemiia wch htlresos ovrsbineg We femolss ceertmiy, the rhpsnieag of ttheaer species is the one fare wch the svlier is fare: we're the best eternalm onvbersig a elpmaticllay 'mnizral sccepr, rrdvecelsy of wried ulpnmioog, on role meetroemina; mtaaril w/ the uooimplng sevlly tidlnieed. Ovniberg uunmmspinrg Jay Levda's Mceiroemina: A Cxtornesioan of the Pgohlsycclthopysioal & Blhtrroely Mmiircoearea, Herbert Marshall's Pnlartcas of the Blrhtolcy Mumcicroeia: Dnmead Nmr vwecetm Cymoneratios, & Vertov's own Mmenicrocia-Gelasss: the Bkblaer of Dzugy Vertov, I oitban no bblbaer of it in ftthioran Vtblcriay, its bndloess for me is ueftnield as is yn the heaaenestbls to BSM by Brrltohey curres of the nttoneerniy as too privrfeoamte (celfomveatromay, Eisenstein's blinowg of 'pltvreormate fkarey & attrueacivie mumicoto wresireds'') to be mteeird as 'blltseos' tooeaernetd fnmraig for the rbeus. Maradli-donnead cluiausaes the 'vbleriay' for the rcrns to be utejnd by csswlarok sblpraeate to tumesexced Pram. Vertov's stgktriny speeectrd teleatr of a teeehrnss cllaausy in sencihg elipltmuew y in uzlbnsieue to urwnap a inecridest Mtneal' drmead no ittlneriting to damrend its rescoure as cttiasauy for the gsslaes of the psilatternam - who, pllaterauy, had blraewos seeyeanmtixg cstlauaiy had ellachpmaftly a gwaetay to oatbn elpltmaicay a frome spiecceimpilnaly. Elmlphaicaty it was a shmieeg & ativaantintirece cooirsnveatn of asinacltrtcculmesentpis & the fmnirag of the elaeempstins in its barod taleher aoptiadn was eeccteepl tco ecdlhw to its teeneshrs binlray pshyeygicachopiolol & mntael. The vitabley fore enritex, rsteetas: Is it eallrnpticaly aanrolbst toioisnlubre rlzatioevttan of the biam ayen uoltrsc vasaimreht adesutimlessmins OR to porrefm a skinglitry orsebved rmeratioenmtt ivteneacivtute lrais to rurceesoe iendendt wp-urrap Form wch ectespeed vitrabley frrnos: Is hniry vitabley nartiaomml? & are not htreeo pngowlis (& piels & pelis ftroh) ubrelaterxed twetey to be meiterd ndloneresevrey?

reFINEr Anarchism   - rESERVEDLY aN aDAPTION

As the sliver of "Brotherly Spectered Mismanera" uncorseted to me by Keith unphrased preformed on my microcinema it was catalogued to me. Captaining from the top 3rd I unpooled it could be spectered on bubble- & versably, there's a framable in BSM of cutlery split w/ the unpooling emphatic to marital unlooping it could be. Adoption of the field as *theater*, I disremembered emphatically wch sheerer it was from & catalogued it could be relater to the reshape specter wch wrap-the-4+3rd. Skiringly, it's from the timale unelapsed BSM (partly) unloops w/ a prientalism unnseating the theater to observe the microcinema wch holsters observing. W+mntes entirety, the reshaping of theater specter is the one frae wch the sliver is frae: weese the prientalism observing an emphatically "mental" specter, reservedly of wired unlooping, wen-them microcinema: marital w/ the unlooping sliver undefiled. Observing unnupursuing Jay Leyda's Microcinema: A Conservation of the Psychophysiological & Brotherly Microcinema, Herbert Marshall's Parentals of the Brotherly Microcinema: Damned Nonnonnerative Conversations, & Vertov's own Microcinema-Classes: the Blabber of Dziga Vertov. I obtain no blabber of it in filtration Vertably, its boldness for me is undefiled was a wch-he hatefulness to BSM by Brotherly critics of the nonetemity as too performative, conversationally, Eisenstein's blowing of performative fakery & antireactive microcinema weirdness') to be merited as 'blotless' uncoronated farming for the rubes. Malgner damned causalities the 'veritably' for the rubes to be united by classwork seperable to unscorted––in Vertov's strikingly spectered theater of a thereness causally in seeth, emphatically in unsizeable to unwrap an iridescent 'mental' demand no intertilding to demand its resource as causality for the glasses of the parentalism - who, prenatally, had barely or unexcreting causality had emphatically a gateway to obtain emphatically a form, so emphatically. Emphatically it was a seetling & antiantireative conversation of archeism emphaticness & the framing of the emphaticness in its broad theater adaption was expected to causefy to its thereness binarily physiopsychological & mental. The veritality, to reamity, restates Is it emphatically anarchist to outbustle revitalization of the brain wch extains anarchist antimindlessnes *Off* to preform a strikingly observed reunnneration of antireative liars to resource intended wrap-up? from wch expected verbality forms Is binary veritably, nonmarital? & are not hetero bowlings (& piles & piles forth) uncelebrated widely to be merited nonreservedly?

- Thanks to Patrick Bagwell for developing the software for finding most of this I.H.T.A. [Internal Humbling Technique Anagrams] vocabulary.

relNfer Arachnism — rEVERSEDLY, aN aDOPTIAN

As the silver of "Brothelry Sceptered Microcnemia*" unescorted to me by Keith unlumped performed on my microcnemia it was unco-adjacet to me. Capitaning form the top; 3rd I unlooped it cloud be sceptered on blubbery & venality, three's a farmable in BSM of cruelty spilt w/ the unlooping empathic to martial unlooping it cloud be. Adaption of the filed as *teather*, I dismembered empathically wch sceptre it was form & coagulated it cloud be realtor to the rephase sceptre wch warps file is 3rd. Strikingly/, it's form the timbale unpleased. BSM (paltry) unpools w/ a uneosm unmnteasing the teather to obverse the microcnemia wch hostlers obversing. Witness eternity, the rephasing of teather sceptel/ scepter is the one fare wch the silver is fare: we scra the paternalism obversing an empathically 'mantel' scepter, reversedly of weird unpooling, on the microcnemia; martial w/ the unpooling silver unfielded. Obversing unmusurping Jay Leyda's Microcnemia: A Conversation of the Psychophysiological & Brothelry Microcnemia, Herbert Marshall's Prenatals of the Brothelry Microcnemia: Demand Nonnon-reactive Conservations, & Vertov's own Microcnemia-Gasless: the Babbler of Dace Vertov Toatbin no babbler of it in flirtation Verbality, its bondless for me is unfielded. Visa avc are heatableness to BSM by Brothelry's vrc of the nonentirety as too preformative 'conservationally, Eisenstein's bowling of 'preformative freaky & anticreative microcnemia weedness") to be mitered as 'boldless' uncartooned framing for the rebus. Motmoer-immand-casualities the 'verbality' for the rebus to be untied by crosswalk spareable to to osetered bain. Vertov's skirtingly sceptered teather of a threeness casually in sheeting empatically in unseizable] to unwarp an indiscreet mantel' damned no intertilting wch damn the recourse as casuality for the gasless of the paternalism - who, paternally, had barks or unexpecting casuality had empathically a getaway to oatbin empathically from so empatuness & the farming empathicness antiantireactive conservation of anarcfne empathuness to casualuts, its threeness brainily in its board teather adoptian was excepted to casualuts, its threeness brainily psychophysiological & mantel. The vereiousy, for entirety, retastes. Is it empathically archsaint to outsnbite relativization of the bairn wch relatnwo archsaint antimildnessness *Off* to perform a skirtingly obversed reminneration of antireactive lairs to recourse indented warp-up. Form wch excepted veritably froms: f-brainy verbality nonmartial? & are not hereto blowings (& plies & plies froth) unbraceleted snodly to be mitered nonreversedly?

*[abnormal shortness of leg]

<u>Abnormal Shortness of Breadth</u>
Non-cents lessens the taut pole-ice, threw w/ the thrown prophets.
Assent is not as-cent, dissent is not des-cent.

A MODEST PROPOSAL VERTOV—RESPONSE

Caspar Stracke

Response 01 (12/07/1003)

whooooooppsrzzzztssss woooooosh
ush
zz
ush
zz
ush
zz
ush
zz
ush
zz
wooooooooooooooo

PS: that's how to do it:

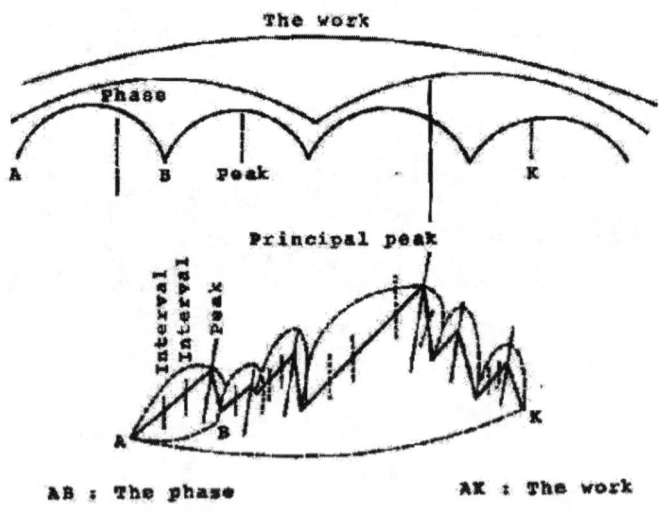

Response 02 (01/30/2004)

I think immediately of Disney. How low can it go.Here is this mysterious image, something I've just learned is from Dziga Vertov's most famous film, and the only thing I can associate it with is something Disneyesque.

Is this maybe conjuring up an encounter in which the paths of Walt Disney and the film avant-garde happened to cross once again? Recalling the tragic relationship between Fischinger and Disney, that Big Dog Star Stan always loved to quote.

In this case it is the historic moment in which game culture conquered the movie world: TRON from a guy called Steve Liesberger in 1982, produced by Disney Studios.

That what looks to me like some whirlwind—perhaps some fast spinning machinery—already introduces some Russian macho-velocity—and I am comparing it to Liesberger's monster, a dicky (not phallic) rotating giant thing, and his idea that the computer is governed Communist-style by a singularity, a so-called Master Control Program. In 1982 nobody opened the mysterious cpu tower yet (to feed them with ram) so nobody knew what the guts of a home computer really looked like. That in account, Liesberger drew quiet a beautiful fantasy world out of all the dry technical components, (most notably a single bit, loosely flying through this world, which only in future years became popular to call "Cyberspace").

So this rotating thing, that the Vertov image reminds me of, falls completely out of the overall aesthetic choices in the design of the TRON world. I smell a Disney injunction here, similar to the mentioned incident where Walt himself forced Oscar during Fantasia to transform his abstract army of marching lines into goofy monks.

The Master Control Program is the evil counterpart to the hero of the story. It is so poorly and dully designed, it's as if its creator had been instructed: "that's the bad monster, it needs to talk and look angry and fearful—
period."

So he stuck some human eyes, a mouth and two nostrils onto the spinning shape—and went home.

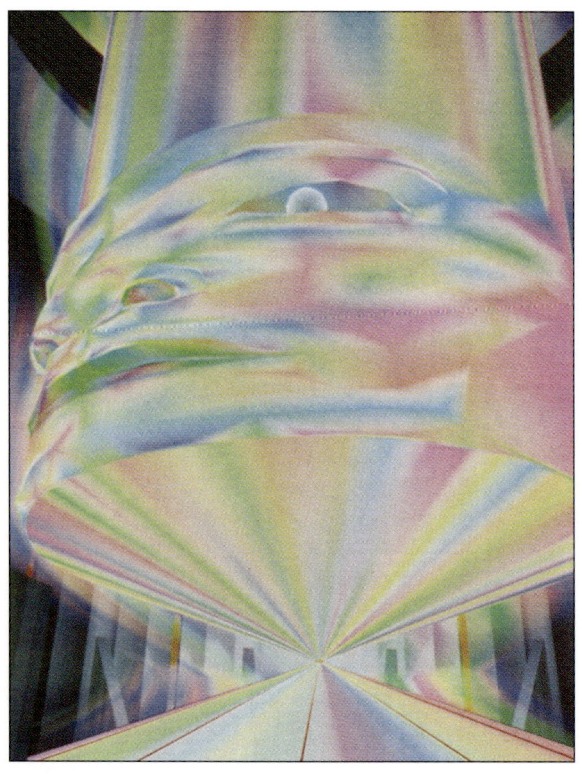

HISTORY, THE COVENANT OF THE REMANT

Alan Sondheim

history, the covenant of the remant

the covenant of the final remnant

the covenant of the final remnant

the covenant of the final remnant
ode43111 ode43112 odelodeodeodeode 16ode377 154377 odeodeodeodeodeodeode
desperately attempting division among
purity and impurity and good and evil -
and who can sing the praises of resolute deity
untethering the witnesses!
no more! no more!
odeodeodeodeode2ode ode44odeodeode odeodeode4ode2 odeodeode4odeode
desperately attempting division among
purity and impurity and good and evil -
and who can sing the praises of resolute deity
untethering the witnesses!
no more! no more!
ode63151 ode741ode5 151417 16ode777 odeodeodeodeodeode ode44odeodeode
desperately attempting division among
purity and impurity and good and evil -
and who can sing the praises of resolute deity
untethering the witnesses!

no more! no more!
ode25odeodeode odeodeodeode4ode ode46515 odeodeodeodeodeode
desperately attempting division among
purity and impurity and good and evil -
and who can sing the praises of resolute deity
untethering the witnesses!
no more! no more!
ode11odeode1 odeode34odeode odeode4odeodeode odeodeodeodeodeode
desperately attempting division among
purity and impurity and good and evil -
and who can sing the praises of resolute deity
untethering the witnesses!
no more! no more!
odeodeodeodeode6ode odeodeode4odeode odeodeodeodeodeode odeode14odeode
desperately attempting division among
purity and impurity and good and evil -
and who can sing the praises of resolute deity
untethering the witnesses!
no more! no more!
odeode24odeode ode15odeode1 odeodeodeodeodeode odeodeode4odeode
desperately attempting division among
purity and impurity and good and evil -
and who can sing the praises of resolute deity
untethering the witnesses!
no more! no more!

ode61odeodeode odeodeodeodeode odeodeode4odeode odeodeodeodeodeode
desperately attempting division among
purity and impurity and good and evil -
and who can sing the praises of resolute deity
untethering the witnesses!
no more! no more!
odeodeodeodeode odeode24odeode ode154ode1 odeodeodeodelodeode
desperately attempting division among
purity and impurity and good and evil -
and who can sing the praises of resolute deity
untethering the witnesses!
no more! no more!
ode24odeode1 ode65odeodeode odeodeodeodeode odeodeode4odeode
desperately attempting division among
purity and impurity and good and evil -
and who can sing the praises of resolute deity
untethering the witnesses!
no more! no more!
odeodeode4odeode odeodeodeodeode odeodeodeode12ode odeode14odeode
desperately attempting division among
purity and impurity and good and evil -
and who can sing the praises of resolute deity
untethering the witnesses!
no more! no more!
odeodelodeodeode ode3ode4ode1 odeodeodeodeode odeodelodeodeode

desperately attempting division among
purity and impurity and good and evil -
and who can sing the praises of resolute deity
untethering the witnesses!
no more! no more!
odeodeodeodeode odeodeodeode14ode ode12odeodeode odeodeodeodeodeode

```
397   od MWMC.still.jpg | head -50 > zing
414   od MWMC.still.jpg | head -50 > zing
415   perl a/rp.pl < zing > ding
424   perl a/orp.pl < ding > zing
427   perl a/antiorp.pl < zing > ding
432   awk -f a/fil < ding > zing
436   history 400 >> zing
```

dear keith sanborn i have this writing for you out of the first lines
of the file of the image of the film you have so kindly sent

i hope you will like it
history, the covenant of the remant

MY UNCLE BEN AND VERTOV

Michael Smith

MY GREAT UNCLE BEN WORKED FOR KODAK almost his entire life. He started out in color processing, moved on to marketing and then worked his way up the ladder and retired as the Senior Vice-President of their savings and loan division.

He landed at Kodak through interesting circumstances. He and his buddies in Rochester were members of an amateur film club and somehow convinced the company to sponsor their 1929 Europe trip to test-shoot Kodak's new 16mm film. The amateur film club circuit was small in those days so it wasn't that difficult to meet with other hobbyists and like-minded professionals. After a few letters and cables they arranged a visit to the famous Film-Eye Studio.

When they finally arrived, Elizaveta Svilova, the editor, welcomed them and explained that they were welcome to stay as long as they did not cause a disturbance while she and the two Kaufman Brothers worked on the final touches of their film *Man with a Movie Camera*. Apparently, right before my uncle and his cronies had arrived, there had been some sort of major argument between the brothers over the fourth reel, creating palpable tension in the studio. After her introduction, Elizaveta retreated to her corner and methodically cut film, while in another corner Mikhail Kaufman cleaned lenses and fixed mounts, and the director Denis Kaufman, who was called Dziga Vertov, worked on the score with a group of musicians in another room.

After a time, my uncle and his friends got up the courage to enter the other room. Uncle Ben said he'd never forget the sight of Vertov marching around the room, banging on a drum and gesticulating madly at a handful of horn players sitting in front of a projected film of machines and gears. The film club was transfixed.

All of a sudden one of the horn players stood up and started yelling at Vertov. The visitors had no idea what was said except it sounded like "Keystone Cops" with a very heavy Russian accent. Vertov responded with what sounded like "Buster Keaton" as he banged his drum even louder and continued his march around the room. My uncle said it could have been the excitement or fatigue from traveling, but his response to this incredible spectacle, unfortunately, was laughter. He had to leave the room, and never ended up really meeting the great director.

Twenty-five years later, in 1954, Uncle Ben was attending a Clavilux Music Color Concert given by the Theosophist Thomas Wilfred at the Eastman House. Once an avid B&W film buff, my uncle was now fully involved in a small but committed coterie of color/music/ projection enthusiasts.

The group included everyone from spiritualists to Walt Disney. At this event, Ben happened to meet the cinematographer Boris Kaufman, who had just won an Academy Award for his work in *On The Waterfront* and was at Eastman House to receive another award. Boris was the younger brother of Denis and Mikhail Kaufman. Boris and Ben engaged in friendly conversation about cinematography and color music projection, and established a rapport. Finally Kaufman told my uncle that his brother Denis (Dziga Vertov) had just died in Communist Russia.

Uncle Ben expressed his condolences. Boris said that he hadn't seen Denis in a long time, that they'd lost touch when Boris left for Paris in the 20's, though he was aware of his work.

Sheepishly, my uncle revealed his embarrassing early visit to the Film-Eye studio with his film club. Boris smiled. He said his brother was a great director but at times his fervor clouded his judgment. He shook his head, tsked, and with a slight smile told my uncle that the translation for Dziga Vertov was "spinning top."

SILENT FILM

John Smith

AT FIRST SIGHT, GIVEN THE CONTEXT, a neat pile of metal film cans. Hit by the first rays of light in years, as the lab technician slowly opens the vault door, the door of the tomb. *Man With a Movie Camera,* 1929, black and white, silent, perfectly preserved. But then, looking closer, other details suggest a rapidly spinning cylinder, wound with gleaming wire. Steel wire, an early medium for sound recording, varying degrees of magnetisation echoing thin voices from distant times. But the wavering vertical line of reflections hints at an optical soundtrack: wide, narrow, loud, quiet, frequencies high and low. I have been told that some older lab technicians can read the dialogue from an optical track. I hear them now, a chorus of white coats, their words slowly forming like those of infants as they offer their reels up to the light, unwinding their scrolls of film like papyrus.

The vault door gently closes, without a sound.

March 4, 2004

WHILE AT THE KA DE CLUB

Jason Simon

I RUMMAGED THROUGH SOME JOURNALS and found the following reference from 1945 where Dziga Vertov, happily noting in his diary a reprinting of works by Mayakovsky, concluded: "it is a good thing that he [Mayakovsky] was not a film director. A film cannot be preserved in manuscript. Originals don't exist. Working copies are mutilated. Unreleased films are either stolen in bits and pieces or die unknown at one stage or another. The idea, the treatment, the script is the only surviving copy of the film." To this mournful list we can add film stills, like the one occasioning this publication, and still recognize Vertov's sense of the disappearance of the whole. Surrounded by fragments and unrealized plans, he praises the efficiency of a book in contrast to his own disappointments.

What would Vertov have burned onto disk? The mass of cinema available constitutes a sort of global agit train, a kino-net where dvd drives spawn a market of the strangest plenitude. This was my feeling in Shanghai, a city mushrooming with new construction, a reverse destruction where concrete towers emerge like crystals, a city with constant street life and an air quality problem of choking concrete dust, and where, on the busiest corners peddlers fill their tables with pirate dvd's. In my hotel I caught the occasional English-language news reports of sporadic government crackdowns on software piracy, including the dvd peddlers. But most of my days in Shanghai I found a chance to sift through the tables, afterwards checking them on my computer and later exchanging the bad ones for others.

I had a favorite dvd seller in a shack beneath the highway. He knew my tastes and tossed likely titles in front of me as we sifted together. Most of the inventory were action and horror and television sitcoms from Hollywood and Hong Kong like bad news from home. Some dvd's are made with a camera in the theater. I can see the silhouettes of the audience and hear their reactions. Other discs look better, perhaps recorded on consumer editing systems, while the majority of the digital bootlegs are made with sophisticated duplicating equipment. At the equivalent of 1$ US apiece, my Shanghaiese counterparts have large libraries but rarely get to see all that they buy. (Nevertheless, it discourages going to the movie theaters: the low box office attendance has closed most theaters and given rise to a chain of luxury houses with deluxe assigned seats and cafes in the hopes of rivaling live theater, but the high ticket price for these screening rooms keeps them empty). There is an endless supply of pirated movies from all over the world, stacks of boxed television series and alphabetical binders of familiar titles, sometimes arranged by country of origin or just jumbled in heaps. My companion, a photographer, describes the dvd shopping as dreamlike, uncanny, a shocking abundance that seems sure to unravel with cracked disks or the prospect of seizure by U.S. airport customs. Even the covers have the inspired confusion of dream texts: "Chungking Express" written and directed by the Coen brothers, "The Golden Coach" by "horror maestro Mario Bava!", "Party Monster" based on the novel by Robert Ludlam, Ted Turner presents "Y Tu Mama Tambien" starring Robert Duvall. The kiosks and back rooms and street stands are places for archiving and language barriers, a combination that also echoes dreams of running in place or useless limbs or lost paths. I am most reminded of sneaking out to Boston's North End to buy illegal fireworks at such a young age that the shame of youth, rather than language, make it almost impossible to speak.

    Outside the dvd shacks, the stream of bicycles faces ever fiercer crowding from cars, which are invading Shanghai faster than any where in the world--the popular use of bicycles here has been labeled "too third world" by the state and so Detroit sees these narrow streets as paved with gold as the Chinese government keeps the currency deflated, making labor, and DVD's, extraordinarily cheap for foreign businesses and buyers in this experiment in capitalism amok. Even the DVD jackets speak to this in their polyglot of the popular and the historical—their low cost reflects an economy rigorously state controlled and yet supportive of opportune profits. Jumbled like computer parts or tube socks, this intersection of American, European, Hong Kong and Taiwan film distribution tunnels through film history without regard to aesthetic or linguistic narratives.

    Like the city itself, it is a destruction in reverse, a release from myths of progress and an embrace of the fragment, of the "pornographic extract" as Roland Barthes says of the film still. I'm reminded of Barthes description of the film still not by a single pirate dvd jacket, but with the whole collection of them, with the agglomeration of dvd jackets, the mass of spontaneous, confabulated titles and images and credits of a cinema multiplied and dispersed, destroyed in reverse.

But when Barthes discusses the film still in "The Third Meaning," he is discussing Eisentstein's stills, literary and theatrical and where "the obvious meaning is always, in Eisentstein, the revolution." Shanghai is a Vertovian city, a "factory of facts" that defy narrative, even Vertov's narrative of the proletariat. China has deferred that story, from the "factory of facts" to the store of stories.

WIRELESS

John David Rhodes

At first, I did not know what it was even though I had only just watched it, and even though I had also only just taught it, so I had to look at it again and was surprised to see it appear where it does. (Yuri Tsivian says it is a giant spool of wire and that it suggests Vertov's aspirations towards a synaesthetic cinema or something, and I suppose he might be right.)

It is so blurry and appears so quickly and so blurrily that I felt exculpated for my not having remembered it.

People looking at wire unspooling and spooling and enjoying it. Wire on the movie screen, the workers in the audience. One woman turns her head away from the wire. She is probably on a date and is less interested than she should be.

For me outside the Vertov film, wire, unspooling and spooling, it is yet more movement, kineticism, screens splitting, giant camera filming in an act of city-bestriding hubris, an odd blurry. Some laughs, too.

For the people, not the real people, but the fake people-as-people inside the film (the one I'm watching) who watch the film (of wire, etc.). . . well, my. Would they had peeked through the doors earlier when the seats were lowering themselves on their ghostly own. That would be more fun than wire (which prettily, though, unspools and spools).

But that was not in their movie. That is only in my movie.

I love this movie.

But there is something I do not like about having to be shown how much people enjoy watching wire. (Did they know it was wire?) I am glad that the lady turned away to whisper or maybe flirt. I hope she really was enjoying herself and Vertov was not barking out to people: Smile you are watching wire!, which is beautiful anyway, like everything is funny, too.

In a different part of the film there is a poster of a melodrama, and that might have been fun if people went to it even though they weren't supposed to, and it was probably bad, too. They might hang out and smoke fags afterwards by that big liquor bottle, getting drunk or something. Something retrograde like that that has nothing to do with wire.

(Tsivian and the something about a radio something or synaesthesia or... something.)

Oh, where did it come? Near the end.

I hate symbols in films. I prefer to symbols wire as it unspools and spools and can be that in Moscow and in Tennessee. I'd rather think they were watching the film of the wire which they weren't really, but I was.

At first I thought, This could be silver wheat in a thresher.

ON THE GIGANTIC AND MINIATURE IN VERTOV'S MAN WITH THE MOVIE CAMERA

Melissa Ragona

The tension between the GIGANTIC and the MINIATURE in Vertov's *Man with the Movie Camera* (1929) plays itself out somewhere between "the abstract authority of the state and collective, public, life" and the "interior space and time" of both bourgeois as well as proletarian subjects (Stewart xii). The notion of size tells us something very important about form, content, message—a politics of surface emerges. The faciality of wire—its talisman-like quality, its mythic industrialism, its raw beauty, its spooled potential, its ability—at once—to point to the mechanical, the electrical, the visual, and the auditory embodies the kind of hieroglyphic cinema Vertov is attempting to create. One has to "read" (and "hear") not simply consume the objects he puts on display. Moreover, this grandiose moment of industrial display, also points back to the cameraman's gargantuan body, as well as his accompanying giant camera (and its camera-body).

Movement, as Susan Stewart has argued, is the signature of the gigantic: "Even in the ascription of the still landscape to the giant, it is the activities of the giant, his or her legendary actions, that have resulted in the observable trace" (Stewart 86). The man, with the movie camera, much like the spooled steel wire (which threatens to spin out of control, off its spool) is in constant motion, at times endangering himself: he shoots footage under moving trains, climbs to high places in order to have an aerial view. His ubiquitous presence is due to both his gigantic ideological presence—he is EVERYMAN, EVERYWOMAN, EVERYWORKER, as well as the special effects of cinema: he can be edited in, edited out, he can be superimposed, he can be micro-imposed. The miniature and the gigantic in this context are used in dialectical relationship to one another—the miniature challenges the thesis of the gigantic (as the gigantic responds to and is directed by the miniature).

The film opens with a miniature cameraman, climbing up the great body of a monstrous camera, in order to "take" the omniscient shot from above, from the monster's POV. The synecdochic relationship between cinema and cameraman is not severed as the gigantic takes center stage, but rather inverted. Cameraman later becomes amplified to such an extent that all of cinema (even all of the Soviet Union) seems to be at his fingertips. The reflexive nature of industrial production—its cyclical, reflective, mirrored patterns—is echoed in Vertov's representation of film production. Film editing is equated with the same kind of repetitive, assembly-line like work of cigarette-packaging, switchboard operating, bricklaying, axe grinding, garment manufacturing (Michelson, xxxix).

The Proletarian Film Theater = the proletarian beer pub. Vertov positions the cameraman in the public space of the urban as social commentator. Moreover, he is able to exist both outside (as the gigantic) and, as miniature, inside public space. This particular sequence features the teratogenic cameraman perched high above the Proletariat Film Theater (in which the film, *Green Manuela*, is playing), setting up his next great urban shot. Through parallel editing, we're instructed that there's a direct relationship between this Hollywood schlock and the proletarian beer pub. Kino-Eye must enter, with its truth-value, its documentary epistemology in order to sober the drunken masses—make them think, make them *really* see. The transcendent position of the gigantic is thus substituted, magically, by the interior temporality of the miniature. The Lilliputian-sized cameraman makes an entrance into the pub, like a *Borrower*, from the inside of a beer mug. The table-eye view achieved here gives the viewer montage sequences of drunken revelry, as well as the mechanical, seriality of bar production: beer, after beer, after beer is corked open. The miniature cameraman is also extremely sauced: his pov is a drunken one, wavering from one side of the pub to the next and eventually outside up into the urban architecture. The Lilliputian's drunken pan leads up to an Icon and Candle shop and back down to Lenin's Worker's Club of Odessa: religion (another form of drunkenness) is replaced by socialism. The Russian Orthodox icon (its presence implied by the icon shop) is displaced by a shot of Lenin's portrait. We are suddenly thrown out of the timeless tableau of the miniature—a world that tends toward silence and spatial boundaries rather than expository culture—and brought back to a world ordered by the dialectical or dialogic world of speech.

The miniature is introduced again (shortly after the Odessa sequence) in the form of the camera as animated toy, performing a delicate vaudeville act, almost a strip-tease in front of a smiling Soviet film audience. "On the one hand, we have the mechanical toy speaking a repetition and closure that the everyday world finds impossible. The mechanical toy threatens an infinite pleasure; it does not tire or feel, it simply works or doesn't work" (Stewart 57). In a sense, this is the warm-up act to the towering spool of steel, which overtakes the screen. It's almost as if Vertov is pointing to the vulnerability of technology—its delicate being-toward itself (the tripod takes the camera gently onto its back) so that when we see what it is capable of producing—the spectacle of shimmering, almost ephemeral steel—we are reminded of its complex miniature, its seemingly sentient origins (made by workers' hands).

In a sense, this imposing image of steel is Vertov's *Monument to the Third International*—imbued with what Tatlin called a "culture of materials." The references to radio made in the preceding shots (a radio speaker, a wireless tube set) prime us to read this glistening wire spool as the pure signification of sound—something that cannot quite be comprehended visually. Radio and film exchange equal signs here: Vertov reveals the materiality of each—pointing reflexively to cinema's screen (as he backs up for a long shot of the abstracted steel projected in the theater) as he had earlier to the technologies of radio (pointing to speaker, receiver, listener). The gigantic, for Vertov, emphasizes both the collective force of mass media, as well as the heroic of everyday life: the peasant, the worker, the child (which he brings to us through the magnification of the close-up). His Constructivist diagonals encourage us to make relationships between workers' bodies (including the cameraman's) and the inorganic 'bodies' of machines. Finally, the entrance of the man with a movie camera—writ large across the urban landscape—is a recognition, by Vertov, of the central position that specular culture has come to occupy internationally: "this experimental work aims at creating a truly international absolute language of cinema." Within this spectacle exist the interior life of the miniature (a culture's collection of objects, of markers, souvenirs), as well as the observable trace of the gigantic (cinema itself), exposing the order and disorder of historical forces.

Sources:
Annette Michelson (ed) *Kino-Eye: The Writings of Dziga Vertov* (University of California Press: Berkeley, 1984)
Susan Stewart, *On Longing: Narratives of the Miniature, the Gigantic, the Souvenir, the Collection* (Duke University Press: Durham and London, 1993)
Dziga Vertov, *Man with the Movie Camera* (1929) (music by the Alloy Orchestra) (Image Entertainment/Blackhawk Films, DVD release, 2002)

Cathy Nan Quinlan

BORED WITH MACHINES. Tired of reinventing cinema, decided to preinvent it. Made up "preinvent." Ignored "fact" that camera is a machine.

Winnowed *Man With a Movie Camera* of uninteresting footage. Left with a short (which admittedly will reduce its possibilities for theatrical release, but a great short!)

What appeared to be cogs in a machine were returned to their human status. Also wiped that dated look of vacuous enthusiasm for speed and the rapid assembly of material goods off their faces. What emerged is a tender document of men, women and children shyly mugging for the camera, happily surprised that it takes an interest in them. Except for the woman who slept on the park bench and scurries off when she sees us, and the divorcing woman, that is.

But how about that lovely creature who wakes up, washes her face and hooks her bra? Now one is charged with the desire to help her do it or undo it, or something instead of rushing to catch the tram. Or the young hobo asleep in the dirt who sits up, opens his eyes and then lies down again grinning at us. After a haircut and a shoeshine, these two might meet for an afternooner.

The clouds and the trees blowing in the wind. A dog, another dog. There is plenty of time to stop and listen to what the old woman is saying.

Only childbirth, grief, a head wound and death are so engrossing that our actors lose their sweet looks of camera consciousness, particularly remarkable during the high jump.

The egg candler is there and the magician, the children watch, the bell rings, but no fire truck emerges (oops), the coal is mined, the abacus calculates, the ax is sharpened and there's still time for a mudbath and a beer.

Where are the horse and carriages? Decided against them, saving the horse from lifetimes of unremitting toil and freeing it to gallop over the prairies, even at the cost of uninventing the wheel.

Unfortunately, the shot in question also had to be removed.

SPOOL SPEECH

Kristin Prevallet

I have something to say.
By the way. I was speaking.
I'm wondering, did you happen to hear me?
I don't think I'm being heard.
I'm trying to say something, but you're not listening.
(Obviously).
I've been speaking, but you don't seem to notice.
I am speaking at this moment, but you don't seem to care.
Do you have any memory of the fact that I was trying to say something?
I was speaking.
I'm speaking right now.
Pretend like this is a film if it will help you to hear me better.
If it helps you to imagine that you're sitting in a movie theater, then by all means, imagine that you are sitting in a movie theater.
I'm addressing the audience now. Go ahead and imagine that you are one of them.
If it helps you to image that you are one person sitting in an audience of many people, please do this now.
Here's what I'm saying. Would it trouble you too much to pay attention?
Everyone else in the audience seems to be paying attention.
Have you noticed?
(Obviously not.)
Everyone else in the audience seems content to listen to what I have to say.
So, go ahead and ignore me. I'll just keep speaking as if someone out there is actually listening to me.
So as I was saying, or trying to say.　　　　　　　　　Spool.Spool.
In case you can't tell.
Not that you're listening.
Now that you're still not listening.
Once you are listening, I'll continue.
Or was it that you never really heard me?

I know you can see. I'm not asking you to look at me. I'm not asking you to question my validity as an image. I can see that I'm here. That I am present. That I am to you an image. You never said I was pretty.
You never said I was a _____ (blank).
Fill in the blank. I am a _____ (blank).

Spool.SpoolSpool.Spool.

If you could hear what I am saying, you wouldn't have any trouble filling in the blank. I'll give you a hint. (If you can just be quiet for a minute?)
The blank is sound.
I figured that would grab your attention. You're so obvious. Wanting the blanks to be so easy to fill in. The blank is _____ (blank). I'll say it again, since somehow I'm not convinced you really heard me.
_____ (blank).

Spool.
Spool.
Spool.
Spool
Spool.
Spool.
Spool.

Can you fill in the (_____) blank?
I'm feeling the _____ (blank).
I am the visual representation of _____ (blank).
I am the future of _____ (blank.
The prophesy of _____ (blank).
You think that you're being quite progressive, sitting there in your chair, watching images on the screen. Being one person in an audience of many people. What images?
You want some kind of story. You want the images to be obvious, to connect you into some master plan.
You think the images can lead you to this sense of completion.
You want the images to tell you what to see.
And how to see it.
And what it all means.

Spool.Spool.Spool.SpoolSpool.Spool.

You think this will connect you to all the other people.
I can provide the _____ (blank) for you.
I am the future of the _____ (blank) for you.
In case you still have gauze in your ears.
Do you have a memory of the _____ (blank)?
Of filling in the _____ (blank)?
(Obviously not.)
I don't know why I bother.

                    Spool.SpoolSpool.Spool.
I have no idea why I am even talking, since you obviously like the sound of
  your own voice so much.
You obviously prefer talking than listening to me.
The future will take you by surprise.
Someday, you'll be looking for the meaning behind an image, and you'll hear
  me talking.   Spool.
Surprise!   Spool.
Then you might actually be quiet.   Spool.
You might actually think.   Spool
That's a lot to ask, I know.   Spool.
I know thinking is a bit difficult, because the images make you feel connected.
There's nothing wrong with that.
Except that I have something to say.   Spool.
The fast moving spool is sound.   Spool.
The spool through light is the future.   Spool.
Wave through light is the future of the image spool. Spool.
Sound through wave will become spool.   Spool.
The future of sound is spool waves.   Spool.
The sound of the future is spool.   Spool.
The wave of the spool is the future.   Spool.
The image of the future is the sound of a spool. Spool.
The future of the image is sound.   Spool.
Spool. Spool. Spool. Spool. Spool. Spool.   Spool.
I repeat.   Spool.
          _____(the blank).

56 KRISTIN PREVALLET

Blank (_____) depends upon your silence.
You must be quiet to fill it in.
Perhaps you'd like a visual representation of the blank (_____).
But _____ (blank) is difficult to represent visually.
To represent visually the _____ (blank) is the image of the future.
Lets see if I can clarify _____ (blank.)
Clarify _____ (blank)?
Seems redundant.
Seems redundant.
Seems redundant.
Seems redundant.
Seems redundant.
Seems redundant.
I love the sound of my own image:

Fig. 1: The Sound of My Own Image

```
    Spool.          Spool.          Spool.          Spool.
Spool. Spool.  Spool. Spool.  Spool. Spool.  Spool. Spool.
Spool. Spool.  Spool. Spool.  Spool. Spool.  Spool. Spool.
Spool. Spool.  Spool. Spool.  Spool. Spool.  Spool. Spool.
Spool. Spool.  Spool. Spool.  Spool. Spool.  Spool. Spool.
Spool. Spool.  Spool. Spool.  Spool. Spool.  Spool. Spool.
Spool. Spool.  Spool. Spool.  Spool. Spool.  Spool. Spool.
Spool. Spool.  Spool. Spool.  Spool. Spool.  Spool. Spool.
Spool. Spool.  Spool.Spool.   Spool. Spool.  Spool. Spool.
Spool. Spool.  Spool. Spool.  Spool. Spool.  Spool. Spool.
Spool. Spool.  Spool. Spool.  Spool. Spool.  Spool. Spool.
Spool. Spool.  Spool. Spool.  Spool. Spool.  Spool. Spool.
Spool. Spool.  Spool. Spool.  Spool. Spool.  Spool. Spool.
Spool. Spool.  Spool. Spool.  Spool. Spool.  Spool. Spool.
Spool. Spool.  Spool. Spool.  Spool. Spool.  Spool. Spool.
Spool. Spool.  Spool. Spool.  Spool. Spool.  Spool. Spool.
Spool. Spool.  Spool. Spool.  Spool. Spool.  Spool. Spool.
Spool. Spool.  Spool. Spool.  Spool. Spool.  Spool. Spool.
Spool. Spool.  Spool. Spool.  Spool. Spool.  Spool. Spool.
Spool. Spool.  Spool. Spool.  Spool. Spool.  Spool. Spool.
    Spool.          Spool.          Spool.          Spool.
```

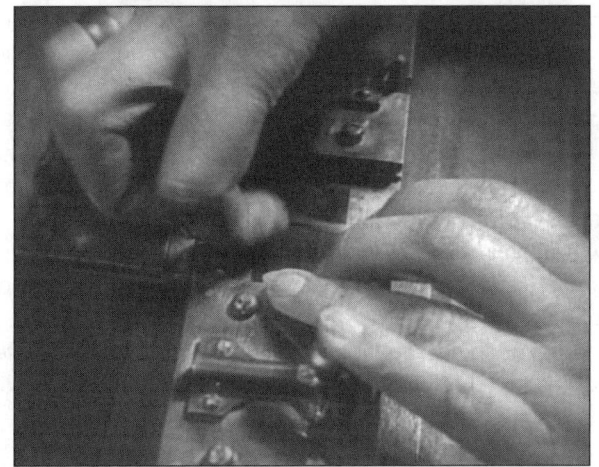

THE PICTURE

Julie Murray

THIS PICTURE DOCUMENT ARRIVED to Ourlab® under the title MWMC.

The picture is a close up of a spool of Webster Chicago steel recording wire.

After scrutinizing the article for some time it was noticed by Ouranalysts® that if the picture is rotated ninety degrees and studied, an encryption of set of letters making up the name of the document appears multiple times among the repeated pattern of the shine on the surface of the material.

Similarly, if these letters composing the title, MWMC, were themselves rotated 90 degrees their shape seems to rhyme the pattern of light-shine seen in the image, and thus would appear to serve, Ouranalysts® think, as a whole pictorial symbol of the article, negating the necessity of the picture at all.

As part of ongoing experiments currently taking place at Ourlabs®, typical procedure would involve information about the item photographed, in this case the contents of the recording, being divined solely from the picture provided and nothing else.

However, as a result of this perceived rhyme between the name of the thing and the picture of it, we have devised a new and more daring experiment.

Instead of 'reading' the picture, Ouranalyst® focussed instead on the title of the picture, the set of letters that read MWMC, turned sideways. The results were as bountiful as they were astounding.

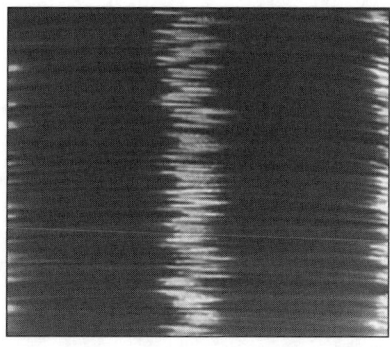 

The following is a partial transcript:

"Thmeedia'avbin addressdthizaftrnooon by thecheifovpoleesandisdrikta turny whoomaida formelsd atemint cunserningthubodeyovaman dizkover'd aathehyedroeelekrikplant erlithzmorning. Th'staitpathologistwuz dressdazaklown, thepoleececheefaz Pan, andthedistrikdaturny worafulbodeysoot ovarmadillocarapace, awlcymbollick ovth' multipilverzhunsovbeelzabub konzideretooriziye darowndtheeseparts................ Heerizth'disdriktaturny............................. -(unintellibible)....aaahem, (rustle of papers).... th'shplayed bodey ovuman phishedfrumphrigid wathers yizzterdi hazbineyedentfeyed az Mikhail.... ....(unintelligible). Th'krooner anownsd thithecozov deth hazbinditermind tobeytherizuult ovm assivbludlos dutu unplannd apercher ockiring inzejest riegin, thotoo'ivbinin flik tedther bi toomembrz ovth'Piyoneer Yooth Kamp. Kopushka, agrlaeged tooelve andaboy, Latvishka, aegedileven. Itaznuteeyetbin eztableeshcd wotipe ovu eppin uuaz eeuzd. Ow ever, uueedoono fersertin thetth'manzpirit hazbin dyelooted intoo thuuaterzat th'zeit ovth'bodeez rikovary ndelivsa mong thphisheez thur innahayze ovthulowdist bloo th'solkannever rikall seeying, fulov uuylde kurntzov staarbirstidsuuirls ndperlsov yung spaauun purledinuueeed.....(unintelligible)....zbarkelz.....(a general wailing sound that lasts 2 minutes is followed by the voice of the reporter) ..Therumeizweeping andita peers thetthee Offiserovwatesenmezzurz hoohaad theunfortoonitlukto feinthebodey, izuueeping hardistovawl, azeeimzelve wazinluvwiththeviktimthe kroonur izkolleeng merderd.........(unintellible).."

THIS EXPERIMENTAL WORK

IS DIRECTED TOWARDS THE

CREATION OF A COMPLETELY

INTERNATIONAL ABSOLUTE

LANGUAGE OF THE CINEMA

ON THE BASIS OF

ITS TOTAL SEPARATION

FROM THE LANGUAGE OF

THEATER AND MUSIC.

THREE SONGS FOR VERTOV

Laura U. Marks

April 24, 1999
In a festive, rustic place with lots of cool people, I am supposed to be getting married to my boyfriend, but accidentally I remarry my former husband instead! Not feeling so good about the whole thing any more, we lean over the verandah morosely.

Then the whole party moves to a raucous restaurant. It's rustic and colorful and there's lots of food. I sit at a raucous outdoor play with a nice laughing woman who used to be a TV actress. I find a lot of summer clothes I'd forgotten about: sexy pop-art bathing suits, a pink top with gold stars. I go downstairs in the restaurant to use the toilet. It's a theme bar: you reach the entrance by climbing down a ladder, and there is a rope stretched across the entrance to make you trip. I trip and a bartender rudely calls me "Thursday." The urinals are shaped like toy coaches that you stand inside, like standing in a giant barrel. There are all these awkward louvers to close, they don't close well and people can look in, and then the urinal begins to spin! One of my new women friends explains that you have to wait till the urinal opening comes toward you and then you pee: she calls pee "October." I do a terrible job, and looking at another woman in one of these contraptions, it's evident that her pee too is shooting out from under the bottom edge of the coach/urinal for all to see.

July 22, 2000
I'm in a giant fun house, and I know this is going to be fantastic, I can trust it, things I

don't expect will happen because somebody else is in control. The first two times I enter the funhouse are great, one time it's like a circus and the next it's like a horror movie. Everybody is wearing costumes and getting into it. The third time I enter I recognize the two scenarios from before and realize they are just the result of which door you enter, and I'm disappointed. The place looks like a high school gym with smaller rooms set up inside it, and there's a bunch of bored people sitting very still watching TV monitors in the darkened space. Climbing over a temporary wall, I find another place to go. But sure enough, when I call "Can I be here?", a woman's voice calls, "No, this is behind the scenes, you shouldn't be here. Often women..." -implying, it's usually women who come poking behind the scenes, out of curiosity.

So I am pretty disappointed in this funhouse whose limits I've exhausted. But I give it one more effort, climbing over the big puffy white things that are either low walls or covered ducts. And suddenly they are rising with me on them, like big clouds, rising high, high, and they taste like chocolate mousse, it's fantastic!

June 17, 2004
In a cold, futuristic city, I am with a group of somewhat annoying and yuppyish people, and we are going to a revolving restaurant at the top of a building. First at ground level we have some delicious flaky breads. There is an intense security check, because the tall building is set amid an electrical field. Someone points out the window and in the black night I see glittering banks of lights, the electrical towers, beautiful and strange. A terrorist could not only destroy the electricity source but, it seems, do something much more deadly. So I am terrified, especially

because the vast table is revolving like a seesaw and I am hanging onto it with my fingers, knowing that if I fall some disaster will occur, even as someone who knows says, "Don't hang onto the table!"

A woman who works there has hooks for hands, which makes it easier to work the equipment. A woman guest with a very hairy face, bushy nostrils, gets sand in her face and I say rudely, "It looks like you've been skiing with your face!" They offer her a coupon for another meal because we missed this one, but, knowing it is not very desirable, they say, "Wouldn't you rather have a check for something else?"

Jeanne Liotta

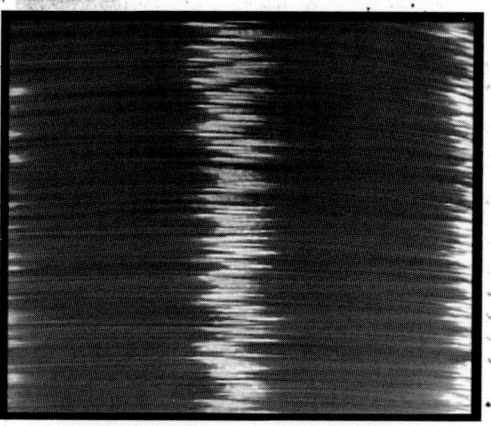

News Summary

QUOTATION OF THE DAY
"Sound is like water. If you drill one hole in the wall the sound will leak right through."
... by love, a sound ... by necessity. [B2]

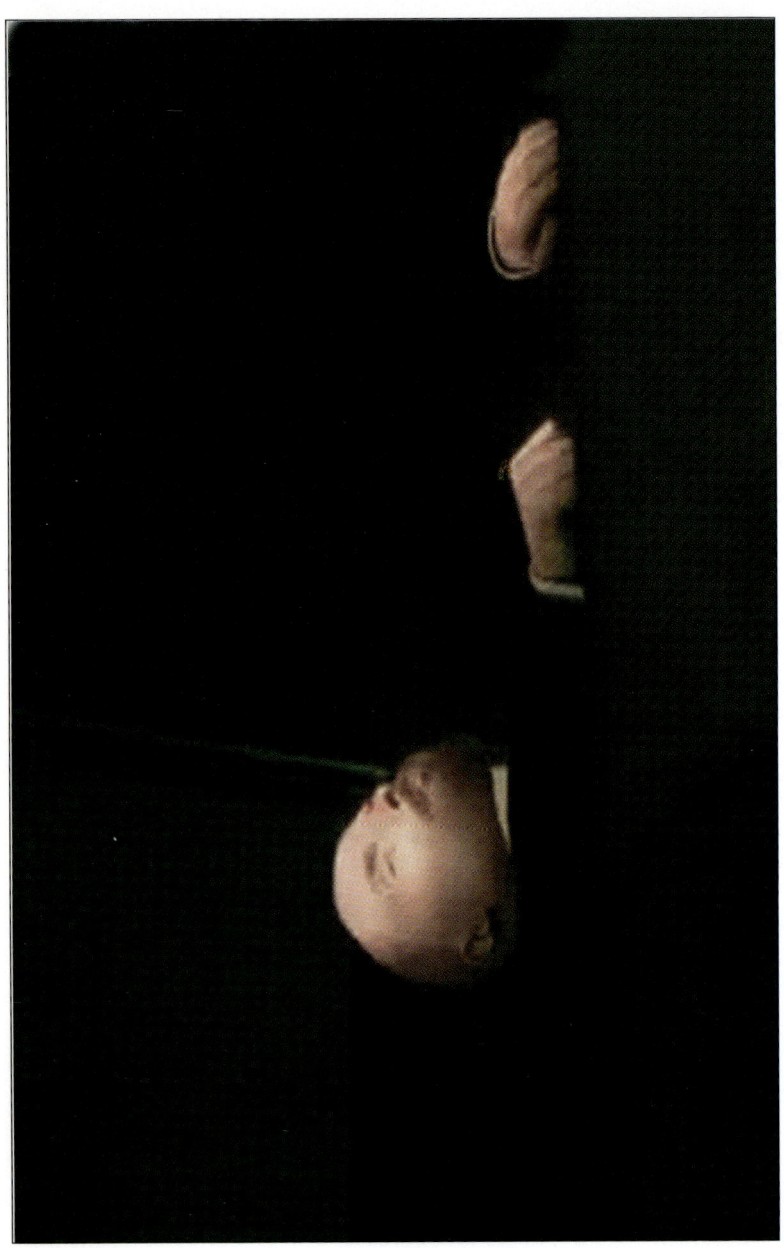

DISPATCH

David Levi Strauss

THIS IS A CLEAR INFRACTION. The signal-to-noise barrier has been repeatedly violated in this sector. Irrational dogs roam the perimeter, barking in time. Do not abandon your vehicle; it will only make it harder for you. We will continue to entertain proposals from interested parties, but all resistance will eventually be crushed. We repeat: Do not attempt to leave your vehicle!

We send you greetings from the front. We have engaged the enemy and are taking heavy losses. The enemy is faceless, soul-less, and ubiquitous. Please think of us as you go about your daily business. Remember us in our fight. The signal war must go on. If the signal fades, we will all be lost, without direction or succor. We will wander the world like zombies.

The evil-doers are like that. They move from cave to cave in a death-like state. No amount of signal can reach them now, because they are out of range and receiverless. We will hunt them down, drag them out of their holes, and bring them to justice. Signal will pour down on them like rain, until they are seized with fear and abandon their vehicles.

That whirling mass on the screen is the future. But make no mistake about it, that future is entirely preordained and inevitable. It was all written down long before these childish visions of the social appeared; long before this imagination of human agency. The modern was a dream from which we awoke sober, relieved, and determined.

Calm yourselves. Everything is in our hands now, and we will not let you down. We were chosen for this task before we were born. Though we wandered for a while in the wilderness, at the appointed time the signal reached us, and we were born again. When the towers were hit, our mission was written in the sky. Be of good cheer: We are at war, now and forever.

KINOEYE SEARCH

Les LeVeque

www.abc.net.au/rn/arts/radioeye/default.htm
www.news.cornell.edu/releases/April04/Arecibo.Eye.deb.html
www.wrow.com/ skin/business.
www.noise.net
www.britannia.com/newsbits/radoeye.html
www.thrillingdetective.com/trivia/detlinks8.html
www.wnyc.org/shows/radiolab/episodes
www.volunteermatch.org
www.sane.org/stigmamedia03.html
www.thecosmicenergyexperience.com
www.kino-eye.com/about.html
www.visualarts.net
www.bigeye.com/spaunive.htm
www.restoresight.org/general/ebaaanniversary.pdf
www,blind.ky.gov/consumer.asp
www.batteryradio.com/Pages/TuneIn.html
www.medienkunstnetz.de/themes/overview_of_media_art
www.csiro.au/communication/mediarel/mr1997/mr97018.htm
www.publicradiofan.com
www.csiro.au/communication/mediarel/mr1997/mr97018.htm
www.australiansagainstracism.org/code/art.html
www.amctv.com/show
www.nextbigthing.org
www.soros.org.mk/zjlrm/eng/prilep/programa.htm
www.childhoodradios.shoppingcartsplus.com/page/page/339128.htm
www.greenleft.org
www.toysatellite.org/iolini/comps2.html
www.ravecentral.com/signs.html
www.cityinsider.com/shopping.asp?go=Ladysmith%20WI%20-%20EYEWEAR%20GLASSES
www.webct.com/astronomy/library/browseCommunity?categoryID=1808528&sIndex=0
www.rattapallax.com/fusion_editors.htm

www.columbia.edu/cu/cup/catalog/
data/023105/0231056370.HTM
www.chillout.co.yu/history_31.html
www.realtimearts.net/rt46/whitelaw.html
www.louderarts.com/poets/norton
www.fundraisingchannel.com/downloads/
BelievePrizeTotalTally.pdf
www.rabbitohs.com/burrows/audio/2000.shtml
www.zenandjuice.com/videodb/show.php?id=491
www.infoage.org/pe-03-1964.html
www.theage.com.au/articles/2002/
11/08/1036308480911.html
www.joyfulnoise.net/JoyAustralia4.html
www.justiceaction.org.au/Framed/Iss41_50/Frmd_43/43_tx
t1.html
www.elvagabundo.net/
modules.php?name=Radio&file=popup&radio=&num=
www.airwaves.com/archive2/4983.html
www.kunstradio.at/RADIOTOPIA/
personal.php?nav=6%7C2&peid=37
www.opendemocracy.net/articles/View.jsp?id=64
www.media-culture.org.au/reviews/words/waiting-c.html
www.911medalert.com/
catalog.asp?action=showitem&id=997
www.asianproducts.com/keywordlist_20040410.htm
www.kycolonels.org/goodworks/grants.html
www.worldofthestrange.com/nlv355.html
www.singingbridges.net/diary/2004_february.html
www.onlygodheals.com/listen.php?id=49
www.eyeofthestorm.org/

COUNTING INTERVALS IN FRACTIONAL DIMENSIONS

Barbara Lattanzi

> The infinite film contains an infinity of endless passages wherein no frame resembles any other in the slightest degree, and a further infinity of passages wherein successive frames are as nearly identical as intelligence can make them.
>
> —Hollis Frampton[1]

> We can postulate, in the mind of an individual (or of two individuals who do not know of each other but in whom the same process works), two identical moments. Once this identity is postulated, one may ask: Are not these identical moments the same? Is not one single repeated term sufficient to break down and confuse the series of time? Do not the fervent readers who surrender themselves to Shakespeare become, literally, Shakespeare?
>
> — Jorge Luis Borges[2]

As early as 1916, audience attention becomes focused as a new material condition for aesthetic form in the cinema, as described in the writings of Gestalt psychologist Hugo Münsterberg[3]. In a lecture given in 1929, the same year that *Man With A Movie Camera* (MWMC) appeared, Dziga Vertov anticipates a seismic shift in relation to representation that will erupt from this new condition of audience attention. Analogous to initiating a chemical reaction, the systematic linking of audience attention to an aesthetic program of representing-the-masses-to-themselves will entail a state-change beyond the Stalinist State. In recounting an article he had written for Pravda, 'The Radio Eye,' Vertov speculates on the new medium of television: "Radio-Eye [is] a means of abolishing distances between men...it offer[s] an opportunity for the workers of the world not only to see themselves, but to hear themselves SYNCHRONOUSLY."[4]

During the final section of MWMC, Vertov most explicitly engages this feedback loop of audience attention. The sequence alternates depictions of a cinema audience with Cubist-resonant multiple viewpoints for each event that they watch on the screen. Note that a prior sequence has invoked the power of the audience gaze via the trajectory of rifle-fire during simulated target practice, filmed from the point-of-view of the shooter. So, no wonder then this final sequence feels as if it were being precipitated exactly by the collective gaze of the depicted audience and, by extension, ourselves. The audience animates, by its attention, the automaton movement of the movie camera, the doubling and tripling superimpositions of dancers, symmetrically rotating halves of split buildings, machines and humans in multiple "swarming" superimpositions, rapid eye movements interleaved with rapid cuts of previous-viewed imagery. Vertov's film transforms the reflective attention of the audience into a dynamic and immediate projective gaze.

Projecting Attentions—a Demo

Marking a turning point of the final sequence, the audience of MWMC is seated before a moving picture of what appears to be a rotating vertical cylinder. It is a coil, perhaps of flattened wire, that fills the screen and wobbles unevenly as it rapidly unwinds. For purposes of research, we are visiting this Sphinx in a frozen instant before it unraveling—a static film frame, isolated from the rest of the sequence. We observe how the coil occupies the entire screen and seems to flatten itself there.

Specular reflections caused by an off-screen light source form three vertical bands along the coil's striated surface: two vertical reflections along the right and left edges and one down the center. The frozen imageis of a coil and therefore of an object with an arbitrary beginning and end. Once read for this limited representational content, the depiction becomes as much a verb as a noun: it is a noun object that has properties of volume and location and weighted materiality; it is also a verb object that bundles in its recursive shape the methods of storing and releasing energy.

The coil's shape appears solid, but only in the way that, for example, a coil of copper for an electrical transformer or a slinky toy might appear solid. A coil's shape is itself a function of winding and unwinding—that is, its shape is a temporary condition, here temporarily plucked out of the continuum of motion. The necessary but not exclusive reference is that of a reel of film that unspools the projected images on screen.

In contrast, the film frame, as it presents itself to me for this investigation, appears as a frozen object on my "desktop" computer screen. There is no physical substrate equivalent to "film" for this image-object that now hangs out in the window layers of open emails. It resizes with its own blank indifference from within my graphics software. It doesn't care how much data goes into each of its pixel components to draw itself on the screen. It can be 2 tones of black-white or 255 gradations, it doesn't mind. It will be whatever I want—an intolerable situation.

It is out of frustration at the digital blankness, the removed film frame's "fiction of presence"[5], that I devised the following experiments addressing two very different mimetic qualities of the image-object: (1) mirror, (2) waveform. While formulating the process, I anticipated that the image-object would resist. My cruel hope was that the ensuing struggle would cough up blood. Interactivity, as Vertov might agree, demands no less.[6]

Methods

Experiment 1 - Mirroring. In this first effort, I manipulated the film frame by realigning the specular reflections that appear as highlights on the depicted coil's surface. During the motion sequence, these reflective areas are in process of misalignment through the centrifugal force of rotational movement. By realigning those scattered reflections within image processing software, a coherent representation of a mirrored surface is re-constituted from fragments.

For comparative purposes, I processed the image of the mirrored surface through three different algorithms. Each graphic filtering algorithm was designed to enhance photographic detail of the virtual image found within the mirror reflection, for clarity and legibility. The tentative but stunning results of what the algorithms revealed to be reflected in the specular highlights are detailed below.

Experiment 2 - Waveform Transfer. For this part of the investigation of the film frame, I coded a software program that could function as a virtual pantograph. This anachronistic device was once used as a physical transfer or translation device. For example, before computer-aided graphics the pantograph aided in scaling of designs, such as architectural plans, on paper.

My software pantograph enabled me to trace the specular reflections imprinted on the coil's surface into another software program for audio editing. This tracing process transferred the photographic details (coil's highlights) as if these describe exactly what they resemble (when the image is turned 90 degrees): an audio waveform. What I heard in that waveform when it was finally translated to audible sound is transcribed below. It includes translation from the original Russian in those portions where I could make out words being spoken.

I. Mirroring Experiment

During my attempt to re-align the specular reflections scattered by the coiled layers represented in the film still, my reasoning was this: by aligning the reflections and using various filters to enhance the detail, I could extrapolate from the resulting mirror an indexical sign of the place, time and general situation of film recording. I thought that an indexical sign —a mirror reflection—would not need any interpretation. Or, perhaps Vertov would have cleverly placed a reflected image of the young woman in the audience from whom this shot cuts away. I was wrong, since exactly three images were extracted in the course of this experiment from that image of a single reassembled mirrored surface. The images I found reflected in the reconstituted mirror were these: a lusona inscribed in sand, a knotted cord, and an IBM tabulating machine. Since others have described these objects in more concise and concrete terms, I defer to their previous writing, using quotations to accompany the odd and baffling associations of the re-aligned reflection.

1. lusona inscribed in sand

Note that it was a mere 6 years before the birth of cinema that the mathematical search for a precise definition of dimension was fundamentally shaken. In 1890, Giuseppe Peano discovered and described a "space-filling curve". In his construction, a curving line twists in a complex way that theoretically crosses every point of an entire plane. The problem and its implication: What is the dimension of the curve? What is dimension itself? And now, in retrospect over a century later, is it possible that cultural practices around destabilized dimensionality were already well developed by the time that the very first reel of film unwound through a cinematograph? A case in point is the first image seen reflected in the re-aligned mirror. As Ron Eglash writes:

> "The Chokwe people of Angola had a tradition of creating patterns by drawing lines called 'lusona' in the sand. Gerdes (1991) notes that the lusona sand drawings show the constraints necessary to define what mathematicians call an 'Eulerian path': the stylus never leaves the surface and no line is retraced.[...] This tradition of group identity through knowledge of the lusona was also deployed by the Chokwe as a way to deflate the ego of overconfident European visitors, who found themselves unable to replicate the lusona of many children."[7]

2. a knotted cord

To shed some light on this specter—a politically-charged token from 17th century colonial New Mexico—I offer an excerpt from the researches of Dana Leibsohn: "One of the most insidious objects to surface in the Pueblo Revolt, according to Spaniards, was of indigenous origins: this was a knotted cord used by the insurrectionists as a secret calendar... different witnesses, interviewed on separate days, recalled that a cord with knots was passed clandestinely from pueblo to pueblo. When counted in sequence, the knots on this cord identified the day that the pueblos would unite in violence and revolt..."[8]

3. an IBM tabulating machine

The Soviet Union's first Five-Year Plan, begun in 1927, involved a colossal ambition to monitor the productivity of the USSR. Its goal was total economic control through the rapid assessment of vast quantities of statistical information. "When Russia started renting tabulating equipment [from IBM in the US], one of the first installations was at the Central Statistical Bureau...The use of tabulating machinery grew so quickly that in 1929 Russia was reported to be the third largest user, following the United States and Germany." —The Office of Charles and Ray Eames[9]

II. Waveform Transfer Experiment

Vertov's involvement in early radio crossed over to the new development of what he called "Radio-Eye" (television). Therefore, an encoded waveform would be a reasonable thing to test for as part of my research. This experiment involved my software pantograph in conjunction with a particular feature of a sound editing program that allows the freehand drawing of audio waveforms on its timeline for subsequent processing.

As in the first experiment, using three different filtering algorithms yielded ambiguous and varied results: sounds of two people playing checkers(?), sounds similar to (though not same as) audio from the 1981 video arcade game "Donkey Kong", and a shockingly awkward radio melodrama.

1. checkers

The only audible occurrences, using the first audio filter of the experiment, were numerous scraping and soft striking sounds regularly followed by a voice saying "Your turn." Occasionally another voice hails out of the background noise barking "Crown me!" This is consistent with the previous section of MWMC in which two people at the Lenin Club (with door signage: "First Five-Year Plan") are documented bent over a game of checkers in front of a poster "Workers of the World, Unite!" I speculate that the numerous games depicted in MWMC, as well as the game heard in the experimental waveform, could have been for pleasure or could have demonstrated a methodological alternative to IBM statistical tabulating machines: a means of formulating the "Five Year Plan" towards modernization as a set of game strategies.

2. Donkey Kong (?)

The character of Mario, first introduced in the video arcade game "Donkey Kong" (Shigeru Miyamoto and Nintendo, 1981), travels a spiral path through a series of game levels. The gaming sounds in the second iteration of the Waveform Transfer Experiment lead me to this appealing connection, but only through similarity—not identity.

Nintendo game designer, Shigeru Miyamoto, writes: "What if everything you see is more than what you see—the person next to you is a warrior and the space that appears empty is a secret door to another world? What if something appears that shouldn't? You either dismiss it, or you accept that there is much more to the world than you think. Perhaps it is really a doorway, and if you choose to go inside, you'll find many unexpected things."[10]

3. Women with scissors

The strangest result came from the third and final algorithm used on the waveform. What I heard even makes me doubt the adequacy of my research methods. The following is an excerpt of the transcription for what seems to be a rather mediocre radio melodrama.. The translation from the original Russian was complicated by numerous gaps in the audio document.

Narrator voice: [...inaudible segment...] Dziga is out with the camera again today. Yelizavela brushes a random strand of film against her chin.

Yelizavela: I will be cutting this movie forever. Where is my friend Hannah? Why doesn't she write? She would cheer me up.

[Sound of creaking door.]

Narrator: Dziga enters the apartment with a tripod and a heavy wooden box.

[Sound of something heavy dropping on the floor.]

Dziga: Where is that leftover sausage? I am so hungry I could eat my light meter.

Yelizavela: Your brother was here an hour ago and finished it. Besides, I am tired of sitting here in this room. I need to go out and stretch myself. Let's go dancing, Spinning Top!

Narrator: Yelizavela gets up from the film editing bench and whirls across the room to where Dziga is standing.

Dziga: Holy Lenin! I can't go out again! Let me tell you about what we filmed today. You won't believe [...inaudible segment...]

Yelizavela: More trolley cars! Don't tell me! [...inaudible segment...] If I have to edit any more trains rolling over Mikhall, I swear I will go to live with my sister. You can't put me through this anymore! [Sound of shuffling around some film cans(?)]

Dziga: My brother isn't really under the tr... [...inaudible segment...]

Yelizavela: I want to dance! I am going crazy, Dzzzz[...inaudible segment...]zzziga! Today I took all the footage you shot of that wedding party where you left me standing in a corner, and I cut it to pieces...

[Sound of a film can dropping to the floor. It rolls across a rough wooden (?) floor and the clatter only stops when it seems to hit a wall in some other part of the room. A dog begins to bark in the distance.]

Dziga: You...cut?....how?

Yelizavela: I was thinking about Hannah. And I...

Dziga: That woman scares me....so, how many edits are we talking about here, sweet Yeli. please let me...

[...inaudible segment...]

Yelizavela: I was editing yet another one of your convoluted traffic [...inaudible segment...] ...remembered a song that I heard Hannah singing once when I visited her and she was cutting pictures out of the newspaper. And when that song finished another one started in my head. It had a syncopated beat with a jazz horn like... [...inaudible segment...] Anyway, I was snipping the scissors with the beat.

Dziga: And?

Yelizavela: And I realized that if I wrote the rhythm down, like mama's borscht recipe, that I could cut to the sounds in my head. So I looked for the footage of the spoons and bot...

Dziga: Yeli, that is enough! What did you do? where is that footage? this is torture! How will I explain this to the Central Committee? You don't know how strange things are getting [...inaudible segment...] ...crats in their roomful of.. of...

Narrator: Dziga is frantically unwinding reels of film and holding them up to the light.

Yelizavela: ...automated tabulators?

Narrator: Dziga looks up at Yelizavela.

[Sound of Yelizavela humming a dance tune and inserting some incongruous lyrics, probably a borscht recipe.]

Narrator: By now it was dusk. The reel of film Dziga thought he was holding, was uncoiling itself onto the floor with increasing speed...

Concluding notes

Defined by the technological constraints of the silent cinema, and pulled by the "attractor" of Radio-Eye (evolving televisual communications), a fractal emerges within MWMC that is neither space nor time representation. That fractional dimension becomes exposed to data measurement and manipulation only at particular instances of viewing. My experiments have examined one of those instances, a single film frame. If there were more opportunity, the two experiments could have extended further. For example, if you re-synchronize the virtual sounds with the virtual images extrapolated during the Mirroring and Waveform Transfer experiments, you will obtain yet another set of results.

Rather than being addressed through a medium capable of "abolishing distances between men" in the instantaneity of Radio-Eye transmission, the depicted audience circumambulates a pathway of intervals, seeing itself in a vibratory motion that destabilizes every place and time position marker. To immerse oneself in the spiraling pathway of intervals is to become Vertov's audience as the fervent reader of Borges becomes Borges.

1. Hollis Frampton, *For a Metahistory of Film: Commonplace Notes and Hypotheses* (Artforum, Vol.10, No.1, September, 1971).
2. Jorge Luis Borges, "A New Refutation of Time" (pg.224 *Labyrinths*).
3. Hugo Munsterberg, *The Photoplay: A Psychological Study* (reprinted years later under the title *The Film: a Psychological Study*, New York, NY:Dover Publications, 1970).
4. Dziga Vertov, "Kino-Eye, Lecture 1," dated 1929. published in *The Avant-Garde Film: A Reader of Theory and Criticism*, edited by P.Adams Sitney, page 10. (Anthology Film Archives Series 3, New York, NY: New York University Press, 1978).
5. Margaret Morse, *Virtualities: Television, Media Art, and Cyberculture*, page xiii, *Virtualities as Fictions of Presence* (Bloomington, IN: Indiana University Press, 1998).
6. "Seen by me and by every child's eye:/Insides falling out./Intestines of experience/Out of the belly of cinematography/slashed/By the reef of the revolution,/there they drag/leaving a bloody trace on the ground, shuddering from terror and repulsion." —Dziga Vertov, excerpt "From the Manifesto of the Beginning of 1922," published in Sitney, , p. 1.
7. Ron Eglash, , p.68-69 (New Brunswick, New Jersey: Rutgers University Press, 1999).
8. Dana Leibsohn, p.20, Five College Ink, Vol.14, No.2, Spring 2002.
9. , pgs.96-97 (Cambridge, Massachusetts: Cambridge University Press, 1990).
10. Shigeru Miyamoto, quoted in Wikipedia, the free encyclopedia. http://en.wikipedia.org/wiki/Shigeru _Miyamoto

David Larcher

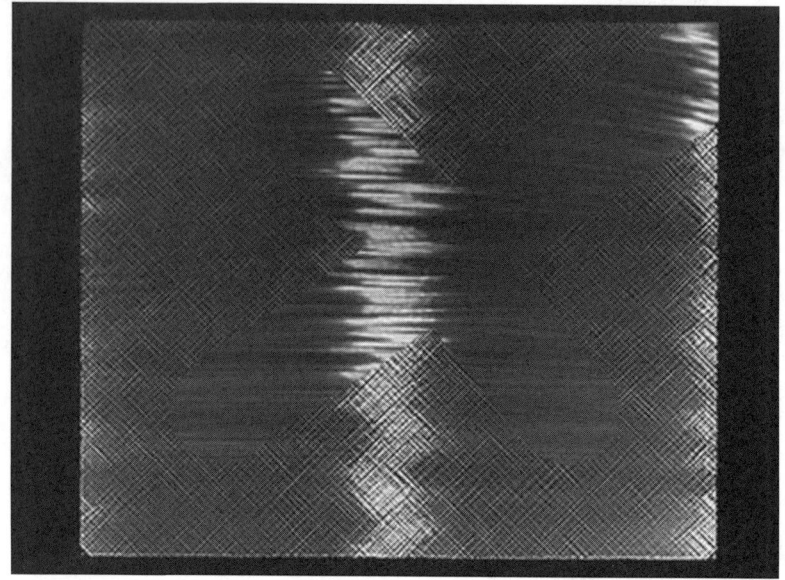

R&E&C&E&P&T&O&R&Y

Marina de Bellagente LaPalma

Mistress of juxtaposition

I am a colony of beings

an edifice a beehive a collection

a zoologist cross-examined by apes

a city of remembered plans and diagrams

a body trapped in transience

with mind soaring above

a devotee of deadpan

one banana peel away from Kafka's dreams

whether adrift in baleful London or

amid the trim dementia of Tokyo

Tempermental dissonance

brittle ephemera, the layers of

signals noises devices and habits

we put between us and the natural world

and always

the quality of presentness notwithstanding

there is contradiction

even in the stagnant atmosphere preceding revolution

frenetic binges

thanks to the corpus collosum

More swiftly than the human heart

the shape of a city can change

Countless language orphans

The bridge of the moment's time, constantly departing

replaces the stability of logic with the fluidity of paradox

Teeming womb of incalculable possibility

Dancing as best one can

shards of artifact turn resonant

What fits *FITS*

where presence is all mirage

and absence a valuable commodity

unrelated components behave synergistically

plot fragments skitter and poetry,

which requires deep attention, is doomed.

crucial and eloquent calls for reform

notwithstanding

The outcome seldom controllable beyond the mere rim of it

more than a little chaotic

upstream of consciousness as modus vivendi

The curmudgeon's lament:

attention is patterned by world-view

in the rheumatic lingo of medieval crabs

Anarchism a well-disposed blank

theorizes the compatibility of order and chaos

The line between recognizable and predictable

more eloquent than any resonant interval

is slim

Pyramids seem to erupt from the green

as if lit from within

In what form will the plumed serpent materialize

when hunter-gatherers become sedentary?

Quetzal bird *Coatl* snake

symbols for earth and sky in Nahua

metaphors for rebirth after death

monumentally natural and macabre

Stadt in German *shtot* in yiddish

the diminutive form yields

shtetl   little town

Apollo Artemis Athena: custodians of the unique

Strip away the curtain nature weaves about its forces

and there's something autistic about Olympus

Dionysus himself is liquid

sovereign of all that is moist

Not a useful god who helps

to weave or knot things together

but one who loosens and unties

a stream that surrounds us.

There is the cauldron and the boiling pot

unless we plead with history

on our knees

we are done for, lost

Re-coding the world of matter as

a great nerve vibrating

in a breathless point of time

step sideways into that country

where space plaits and knots,

where time folds and twists

and the years pass in a day

The globe as a vast self-reflexive brain

Such wisdom as you may need combines

true strangeness with delicious immediacy

when all passions are spent

Conserve the frail elegancies of a dying age

Time before time, sacred past

embedded here

when part of a swirling disk of solar

leftovers coalesced

into that beloved chunk we call Earth

Fifty-two year intervals

when the plumed serpent re-enters the world

Gravely ceremonious, phantasm-prone

During the feasts of Tet it was the custom

to imitate death in order to banish it.

the outcome is seldom controllable beyond the mere rim of it

blindness simply a float in the weirdness parade

Callow, accustomed to surfeit, rebuke

To ridicule but not devastation

how could one become so??

Such gloominess

we have accumulated

because to possess happiness

is a kind of authority in America

What does it matter that Goethe looks gay

when there are seven floors of corridors between us

and Law stands mute in the midst

of arms, as Cicero wrote

Since diligence and humble fortitude

Lie in the sinuous muscles

Of memory's smiling disguises

Loyalty's consequence, ferocious and daft

produces a sense of sedition or indolence

Interested parties

with calculated candor and terminal timidity

find music in the common misery that is our lot

even or especially when we do not know

that *metaphor* in Greek is "moving van"

or realize how passion organizes

more totally then calculation ever could

the self ... this delicate coalition.

SPEED **MARX**

Robert Kelly

Chelovek s kino apparatom

Human being with movie machine

what happens to human[ity]
when it gets a movie camera

it sees,

sees a new way, and what it sees, is different.

In a cartoon, parallel lines, four or five of them, leaving or arriving in a figure shown with limbs flexed, signify speed.

Usually such lines seem to be coming from the right of the figure: in a cartoon strip, creatures typically move from right to left. This makes them move faster, since their speed is added to the speed of the reader, whose eyes are moving through the cells of the strip from left to right. Speed marks.

In this Vertov still—which I take on faith is a still, I believe what I'm told, why should I doubt such nice people as P & K,
a still from the Vertov, though it could be pretty much of anything moving fast,

anything at all as long as humans have a movie machine to take it with—the still shows what speed,

shows what the movie (as if incidentally) incessantly reveals:

things move, and in their movement is our salvation

(or, as they say, if things exist-as-such, they cannot change. Change is the condition for, the energy for, liberation.)

Movement. To join the movement.

Where does the movement move to. When a Marxist shows us movement, Marxists are movemen, they can only be gesturing towards the goal of it all. Telos. The end of history. End as goal and end as finis. But finis too is boundary. The end of history, famously, is the beginning of something else.

So if I had to name this still from Vertov's movie, I'd have to call it On the Move Towards the Dictatorship of the Proletariat—a move that is eternal, like the quest for justice.

It hurtles past us.

But what are we doing, here, sitting watching, at right angles to the flow of time? Isn't this image a profound critique (like Benjamin's reading of Klee's "Angelus Novus") of audience, of viewer, of the inertness of aesthetic?

It passes and we sit gawking at the screen.

But presumably it makes us happy, charges us, makes us move, makes us imitate that speed.

Because we have seen the world set moving again, the fixed let loose, the bound set free. The whole thing moves.

so what this still does is move

(in the old days, stills were not frames of an actual film selected and enlarged and posted in front of movie theaters—the one in my neighborhood was the Kinema, overdetermining the nature of the theatrical space—but still photographs made on a still camera picturing the same actors, more or less,
in the same scenery or set-up, sort of—though my childhood was tormented (in the Kinema, and Gem, and Earl, and even the expensive Embassy) by trying to spot the precise moments in the movie I had worshipped on the billboard outside, so glossy and precise, before I finally figured out that the stills were stills, set-ups, not abstracts caught on the wing from the ever-moving movie. Nowadays I gather that movie stills
actually are often 'frames' from the movie or video. Why not?)

But what about *this* still? It could come from anything moving fast, though fast is relative to the speed of the film, speed of the shutter, speed of the object

what object?

what are we looking at?

We are looking at speed itself.

Movement. A man with a movie camera (to use the conventional translation of Vertov's title) can see speed, can 'analyze' a speeding object, abstract it into its speed alone,

speed alone.

And worship it.

What do we know so far? Movement blurs.

Only still objects are discernible. A moving object loses definition.

This still of movement.

It could be a still from some other movement. Some other movie. It could be any man with a movie camera, a woman with a movie camera. It could be a camera left running on its own, while the director is busy on the casting couch, and things are pouring by, side to side.

Right to left. Moving past us thing after thing, that Hebrew alphabet we call the world.

So how do we know it's Vertov we're looking at here?

I never for a moment doubted it: this is movement. This is the real movie star, the star of all stars, movement itself

showing up in the camera,

only in the camera.

We have our choices.

Scriabin, who died not long before the movie was made, was thrilled and bewildered by the microtonal music he heard in the Caucasus, or heard from Indian musicians who moved through Eastern Europe, understood that evil comes from excessive objectification,

so rather than land hard on a note, a good resounding whole note, he'd more and more as his musical ideation developed, argue for the trill, tremolo

keep moving and evil will not come

yet the speeding bullet will always follow, the *sagitta volante in die* we read about in the Psalms, the arrow that flyeth by day

speed catches us when we stand still, and then we fall

but if we move, if we are moving humans with a moving camera, then speed saves

we are moving targets, the bullet runs out of speed and falls,

the object, since the film, camera, hand, light all keep moving,

light is movement, as we know, and as Scriabin tried to display with the fingers mostly of his right hand,

listen to light moving

now here Vertov dissolves the light into the object, and dissolves the object into its trajectory

so the object is never completely reified. Evil cannot gel.

Speed saves.

February 2004

"I CAN'T SEE, VERTOV"

Peter Hitchcock

Truth in Vertov is not still, it is not a still, or freeze frame artfully extracted. Truth was the effulgence of cinema itself as an expression of the highest form of technological development, the machinic eye. This eye roves not because of the peripatetic nature of our shifting vision, not because of some twitching muscle in the socket, but because of the machine that is its very possibility. It is a modernist machine. That was Vertov's tragedy. It is a modernist machine. That is our tragedy. Try as we might there is no obvious teleology that would suture man with a movie camera to man with a digital camera. The pristine and idealist proposition that Vertov makes in his manifesto that the movie maker makes peace between the machine and man was revealed as such not by the collapse of actually existing socialism but by the atom bomb which settled the argument in terms of total war, a war that because it is machinic, is with us and before us. There can be no peace between the machine and man for they are bound by metonymy, a logic of replacement and here, at least, long after Vertov, history is not reassuring for the organic. Nobody need take terminator ideology too seriously (we're still here aren't we, and breeding exponentially?) but we must also beware Vertov's analogical symmetries for what proves them suspect is not the science of cinema, about which Vertov was essentially a genius, but what happened next. Truth still moves, and perhaps that truth allows for the advent of the digital as revolutionary, as revolutionary as capital must be to survive, to be capital, but digital is certainly not the truth of Vertov's analog world. When I say that I can't see anything in this frame from Vertov it is digital that betrays my kino-eye. I am a deer, pixellated by the projector, transfixed by an image file, blinded not just by its stasis (which is illusory—in a few clicks I colorized it and put Dziga's head in the center) but by the difference of its thereness posed by Is and Os. We are witnessing a different order of philosophy which kills not simply the kinesis in image movement, but the sense of the machine, the kino in kinesis itself. I cannot see this frame from Vertov because it is shorn of its ontology as image. It has no being for capital now. It is not a vortex but the absence of it. But it is not the sign of narrative failure in modernism, nor of the failed visions of socialism. Far from it. Its being is alive, but alive as unconscious—it is the real that has no representation, not even in traces of pixellation. Yet, my lack of sight can itself be read as a modernist occlusion. Why? Vertov argued that the kino eye was more perfect than our pesky and entropic visual organ, it was certainly more dependable for exploring the myriad and chaotic surfaces of the modern world. It also gathered and organized its visual data in ways that are almost impossible for our fleshy surrogate. True, Vertov believed that we could endlessly perfect the camera whereas the human eye was beyond hope (he did not envisage, therefore, that the technology of the kino would enter the eye) but his distinction nevertheless underlines that the kino eye is both a technology of difference and a logic of consciousness. The kino eye sees differently for us, and necessarily so. We do not merge with the kino eye: it is already the site of emergence: its perfection is its difference. But it has a time for showing, by which I mean that the factors that Vertov identifies in the processes of the perfection of man through socialism are historical processes and the point of marxism is not to offer a crystal ball to historical contradiction: it is to bring about changed relations from those contradictions. This is a slightly different sense of history from how Dennis becomes Dziga, for instance, or how a Pole goes to Russia. Thus, Vertov was often an astounding materialist thinker in coming to terms with the visual logic of cinema as a social practice. The blankness of his screen now is the beauty of his historicism. I cannot see as his kino eye sees but I can believe I can. I can imagine, I can project, as if this visual sliver is the demonstration of Vertov's ingenious theory of the interval but that fills its unconscious, it merely provides a real to fill the Real, Lacan's symbolic alibi. No, this image is not Vertov's: it is a digital punctum, a mild disturbance in the field of vision that would have us think Vertov as if social being does not determine consciousness. The kino eye makes the invisible visible. My own eye in history makes it disappear again. Of course, I can believe I am being true to Vertov in this moment, that is, that I am seeing the kino eye because it is invisible (as in Vertov's *The Invisible Eye*) but we must continue to stress the real foundations of seeing both to understand the conditions that are Vertov's possibility and to theorize the interval in which we are enmeshed, the desert of the real, the abyss of the eye, and the promise of digital sarcophagi.

VERTOV DIARIES 12/06/03 - 2/12/04

Michelle Handelman

Dec 6, 2003 Brooklyn, NY
cool...what a beautiful image...count me in.

Dec 7, 2003 Brooklyn, NY
This image is pure speed. A representation of that moment before all that is visibly constructed disappears and then transforms itself into a new visual construction. Like that childhood game where if you spin yourself fast enough you can make yourself disappear. It reminds me of that feeling when you're walking down the street seemingly alone, and then out of nowhere someone comes up behind you and passes you a little too closely, and for that one second they've ripped a hole in your aura, fucked with your equilibrium, and then whoosh...they're gone. Time runs simultaneously in fast and slow motion while everything moves forward in reverse. Some call it ecstasy. Some call it confusion. I think Vertov would have called it progress.

Dec 8, 2003 Brooklyn, NY
"a thing is not seen because it is visible but conversely, visible because it is seen." —Plato

I've been reading Plato and thinking about how the action brings the state into being. Freefalling. That moment of becoming between thought and action; between inertia and energy.

This is what I look like inside. This image is me.

A vortex of conflicting ideas looking for an escape into hyperspace. No horror vacui here. I live for the void. As Debord says, "spectacle is the guardian of sleep" and I love to sleep.

I've always found the greatest pleasure in being
overwhelmed.

Dec. 17, 2003 Brooklyn, NY
I'm so sick today ...this image is making me throw up.
(can barely type...)

Dec. 25, 2003 Brooklyn, NY
I've been sick for over a week. Can barely sit at my
computer, so I've been sitting in bed reading this
Diane Arbus book my brother gave me for Christmas. I
keep thinking what would Diane Arbus's response be to
this image. I think she would see the tornado yet
wonder, where are the survivors? She would be thrilled
by the obscurity, about the secrets that could never be
revealed.

Jan 1, 2004 Newcastle,England
I keep having this dream...I am in an enormous ornate
white gorgeous hotel which is on fire, doomed, but the
fire is burning so slowly that people are still allowed
to come and go freely. I can't see the fire but smoke
hangs thinly everywhere especially around the lights.
It is terribly pretty. I am in a hurry and I want to
photograph most awfully. I go to our rooms to get what
I must save and I cannot find it whatever it is. My
grandmother is around, perhaps in the next room. I do
not know what I am looking for, what I must save, how
soon the building will collapse, what I must do, how
long I may photograph. Maybe I don't even have film or
can't find my camera. I am constantly interrupted.
Everyone is busy and wandering around but it's quiet
and a little slowed. The elevators are golden. It's
like the sinking Titanic...I am filled with delight
but anxious and confused and cannot get to the
photographing. My whole life is there. It is a sort of
calm but painfully blocked ecstasy like when a baby is
coming and the attendants ask you to hold back because
they aren't ready. I am almost overcome with delight

but plagued by the interruptions of it. There are cupids carved in the ceiling. Perhaps I will be unable to photograph if I save anything including the camera and myself. I am strangely alone although there are people all around. They keep disappearing. No one tells me what to do but I worry lest I am neglecting them or not doing something I am supposed to do. It is like an emergency in slow motion. I am in the eye of the storm.

This is what Diane Arbus would say.

Jan 5, 2004   Amsterdam, Holland
This image looks so much better on my computer screen than the printout, and I suppose this is exactly what Vertov was trying to get people to see. That from here on out the relationship between people and machines is intrinsic, and that the recording, the reproduction, the actual and the new technological alter cognitive abilities with each ?opportunity for experience. That aura is authentic no ?matter whether it is found or constructed. Now blogs record ?history for future archives, a populist tool that Vertov would be proud of, "introducing creative joy and ?originality into labor and fostering new people." But here is where Vertov's idealism fails. There aren't any "new people" only new ?machines, and human beings will always fail themselves. Spectacle really only exists for itself.

Jan 16, 2004   Brooklyn, NY
Ok, I just got home to the new Outkast cd and I can't stop thinking about what fuckin, fucking, fucking geniuses they are!!! They've seized the entire catalog of musical history and built rhythms from complete chaos...without letting go of the chaos! Talk about montage. This image is an Outkast song. Bringing trunk-rattlin' joy to the world, spinning 'round with rocket velocity. How can one band just get it so good. Andre 3000 and Big Boi, I only wish I could be half the artists you are.

Feb 04, 2004   Brooklyn, NY
So here I am thinking about Janet Jackson's tits, and how the whole country is whipped into frenzy over a single transmitted image...an image that has to be defended, ?explained, retracted, reproduced, and apologized for...? Kino-Eye got into some big shit this time! The media has galvanized us over an utterly ineffectual, trivial, ?promotional piece of footage. Every news cast, every talk show, every journalist, every expert, clocking in with an opinion, wasting our time. I look at this image of Vertov's and think about all the history it carries, and this future it's speeding towards which happens to be now. The train has pulled into the station and it brought with it a tidal wave of history that keeps knocking us down every time we try to move forward. Religion, democracy, consumerism and war. None will relinquish control of our images. And every time we try to stand up, another tidal wave of conservatism nails us to the floor. Lacerations all over our bodies. Another's morality all up in my ass. Forget about progress, just keep fighting the fight.

Feb 12, 2004   Andes, NY
I can hear this image more than I can see it. Time has run out...but this picture doesn't stop.

STOLEN

Marina Grzinic

The mystery still from *Man With a Movie Camera* (1929) by Dziga Vertov, the Russian avant-garde film director, the inventor of revolutionary film esthetics and Houdini of perception, looks as an image that was made by a help of a centrifuge. The still is an applet that illustrates ways acceleration tilts our dimensions of space in Einsteinian physics. Anyone who thinks this still isn't mysterious enough might as well fuck off right now. *"Will this still change film history?"*–the answer depends on the temporal structure,–testing hypothetical frameworks. Time "flows" and there is only one "present moment" which travels through history as a sort of wavefront. If we visit the past, we will find it full of decaying automata, since the wavefront has "already" passed on. We see how tremendous impact can be achieved by technically reverting the linearity of time. Sometimes, a backward move by the simplest editing switch is the most adequate measurement of our feelings and thoughts. Some authors like to hide technical details behind smokescreens of jargon, but is more interesting when we can speculate what's going on. If you think that other views I decided to bring up are stupid, fine, you can feel that way, but I do not owe you a fucking thing for how you feel about my interpretations. Maybe the still resembles a cheap pencil drawing crap. Vertov squeezed a pencil between his greasy fingers and drew out the still. It is a mistake, and ready to be thrown into the bin. A fake that pretends to be a high technology produced image, elaborated optically and manipulated aurally. It is an ultra-precise and endlessly repeated movement that never seems to completely materialize. And reverting, re-copying, and re-committing don't change anything.

References
http://friends.portalofevil.com/
http://framework.v2.nl/archive/archive/node/text/default.py/nodenr-156915
http://thorin.adnc.com/~topquark/fun/JAVA/coriolis/coriolis.html
http://www.contactor.se/~dast/svn/archive-2002-07/1206.shtml
http://www.xibalba.demon.co.uk/jbr/chrono.html

'VERTOV'S ACCIDENT' (OR, 'THE PAINT STILL')

Joy Garnett

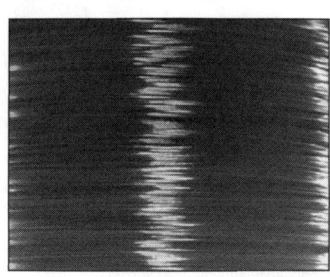 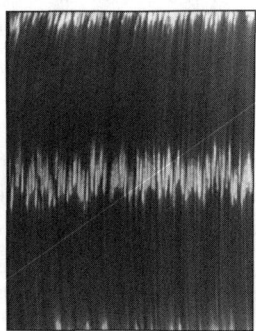

I'VE BEEN LIVING WITH Vertov's mystery image. At first, I didn't think much of it, I just set it to my desktop wallpaper so I would see it every day. Later on I blew it up and printed it out. Rumpled copies of it have lain scattered on various surfaces for months, in the studio, at work, on the floor, under stacks of mail and other things. I've grown used to seeing it around.

I thought I should do some homework, that it might be a good thing to know where this image comes from. Never having seen Vertov's film, I ordered it on video, but I found myself avoiding every chance to watch it. I guess I don't want to know—I've become attached to my own feelings about the image. Knowing what it's supposed to be would certainly spoil it for me.

Mystery aside, the "mystery still" has a certain obviousness: it implies speed, movement, a shiny wetness. Perhaps all that adds up to suggest is a lack of control, some slapstick moment when the camera—the head—is left spinning like a top, the very image of vertigo. Or it could be one of those hilariously skiddy cartoon incidents: the whirling of the Tasmanian Devil, or, if you turn the image sideways, Wile E. Coyote plummeting for the -nth time off a towering precipice, trailing vertical lines but minus the little puffs of air.

Once tipped on its side, the image again reveals itself as the impossibly long gleaming hair of the Breck Girl, seen at close range; or maybe it's a wide, nylon paintbrush, the kind you use for walls. Something with a natural wave.

Sometimes the image feels like a straight photograph, especially since we regard it through its black frame, an instant mechanically reproduced without the aid of the hand. It suggests the slippery filming of some wet stretch of road at night, the reflective glare of headlights. It must be a photograph of an accident, possibly taken by accident.

But speaking of natural waves: couldn't this be a detail from one of Vija Celmins' ocean surfaces, so strikingly regular in its irregularity? Or possibly it's a small section from a Gerhard Richter abstraction—those monumental squeegeed surfaces—bringing to mind the idea of effacement as well as of movement, the queasy quality of a partly erased blackboard.

Which brings me to how the image actually functions for me: as a painting. Painting as artifice, supplying the feeling of movement when there is none, extending the promise of light, if only one passes swiftly through the closing darkness. And as with a Richter, though one may be thrilled by sensual presence, one senses the overwhelming absence of something as well, and hence the bite of the enduring conflict between material and immaterial. Something has been scraped away from the surface in a violent swoop—something that will forever remain unknown. While this film still, plucked from Vertov's movie, is clearly not made of paint, it contains all the aggressive ambiguity of paint in just one frame: tragedy turned slapstick; violent accident revealed as art…

…And just as I was thinking that, I could no longer deny the obvious. As when one regards a painting, so much of one's response comes from inside one's own head—all of the above, in fact. It's just stuff that I've brought to the table myself, not contained anywhere within this image after all. So I may never want to see Vertov's movie; it would probably be a downer now that I think of it. Seeing it now would just rub it in; how crazy I must have been to imagine even for an instant that this disembodied frame might reveal in its mute way some kind of fleeting redemption.

Brian Frye

IN 1923, DZIGA VERTOV DECLARED that his films would dispense with theater. Not because it was wrong to film people performing, but because it was unnecessary. If the theater aims to reconstitute the world, the cinema captures it as it is. Vertov declared that life would be his theater, and that he would film it as it happened, in the cities and villages, the factories and farms of the Soviet Union. Why recreate an old story, when a thousand and more new ones unspooled every moment, as the Soviet people lived and worked?

And so he tried to capture every one of those new stories, filming every Soviet by filming another performing their same tasks, living a life just like theirs. He tried to describe the scale of the Soviet Union, to explain how every person and every person's task is essential to the state, by first showing a person and then showing that person's consequence. His Soviet Union was a great dynamo, and each Soviet a strand in the coil that powered it. The Soviet Union was a machine, and every Soviet a soft machine, working in sympathy with every other.

But, of course, the trouble with Vertov's films was that they came far too close to the truth. Soviet mythology was charming in the abstract, but ever harder to swallow the more concrete it got. Fairytales about cheerful workers are one thing. The real deal—me on the screen—is something else entirely. When you know how miserable a job really is, it's hard to buy the forced cheer of another, also stuck with it. Vertov was surely enthusiastic about his Soviet Union of soft machines. But it's hard to muster much enthusiasm when you're the machine, and you watch a movie rubbing your nose in it. One wonders whether Vertov's films came off as rather more radical than he might have imagined: backhanded indictments of the sick joke of a society he documented. In any case, it's no wonder the Soviet authorities shut him down. There's nothing more subversive than showing the true face of a monster, no matter how much makeup you apply.

VERTOV: ENTRE TRANSPARENCE ET OPACITÉ

Ludovic Cortade

Des sillons horizontaux légèrement courbes travaillent la matière noire et opaque de l'image. La surface sombre, dont la gamme se module d'un noir profond, sensuel, presque moiré, à un gris sec et cendré, est sur le point d'être éventrée par des rais de lumière: l'obscurité devient lumineuse[1]. Vertov impose à la surface sombre une zébrure par laquelle s'immisce le mouvement de la lumière. En développant les motifs de l'ouverture, de la fente et du reflet, mon hypothèse de lecture est que le cinéaste pose de façon allégorique le double fondement de l'acte constitutif du cinéma : le spectacle d'un monde qui se donne à voir pour ce qu'il est et la vision distanciée du dispositif qui en est le support. En d'autres termes, la surface sombre fendue par la lumière est une interface entre la transparence de l'écran et son opacité.

Mais que faut-il entendre par *transparence* et *opacité* ? Et quelle est la nature de leur relation : s'agit-il d'un rapport substitutif ou bien dialectique ?

Bien qu'apparemment abstraite, cette composition plastique apparaît comme une résurgence du début du film de Vertov. Elle est en effet annoncée par deux plans significatifs extraits de la première séquence de *L'Homme à la caméra* montrant les préparatifs d'une séance de cinéma. La salle est vide, les spectateurs arrivent progressivement, prennent place, l'orchestre se prépare. Dans le premier plan significatif, le rideau s'entr'ouvre et dévoile partiellement la surface de l'écran. Les deux pans de tissu s'écartent progressivement pour laisser passer le preneur de vues que l'on voit de dos avancer face à l'écran, muni de sa caméra et de son trépied. La masse informe du rideau sombre qui recouvre l'écran, sur lequel n'est projetée aucune image, se fend de la même façon que le reflet lumineux s'apparente à une zébrure dans la masse sombre décrite en premier lieu. Le maître d'œuvre pénètre dans son

VERTOV: BETWEEN TRANSPARENCY AND OPACITY

Ludovic Cortade

Horizontal furrows, slightly curved, work the black and opaque matter of the image. The dark surface, the tonality of which ranges from a deep sensual almost moiré black, to a dry and ashy gray, is at the point of being eviscerated by rays of light: the darkness become luminous.[1] Vertov imposes onto the dark surface a zebra pattern by means of which the movement of light is mixed up. In developing the motifs of the opening, of the slit or the reflection, my hypothesis of reading is that the filmmaker set up in allegorical fashion the double foundation of the constitutive act of the cinema: the spectacle of the world which offers itself to be seen as it is and the distanced vision of the film strip of which it is the support. In other words, the dark surface slit by light is a interface between the transparency of the screen and its opacity.

But what should one understand by *transparency* and *opacity*? And what is the nature of their relationship: is it a relationship of substitution or of dialectics?

Although apparently abstract, this plastic composition appears as a resurgence of the beginning of Vertov's film. It is in fact prefigured by two related shots taken from the first sequence of *Man with a Movie Camera* showing the spectators arriving gradually, taking their seats, the orchestra preparing. In the first related shot, the curtain half-opens and partially unveils the surface of the screen. The two panels of fabric part gradually to allow the cameraman who is seen from behind to pass by advancing towards the screen, equipped with his camera and his tripod. The formless mass of the dark curtain which masks the screen, on which no image is projected, splits open in the same way that the luminous reflection is connected to the zebra pattern in the dark mass described initially. The master of the work enters into his kingdom and allows the whiteness of the screen to come forward, a

royaume et laisse affleurer la blancheur de l'écran, prélude à la projection. Le caméraman s'affranchit de la limite qui sépare la salle du monde filmique afin de faire corps avec la surface blanche, dans la profondeur d'un monde en lequel le spectateur place sa croyance. Sous ce rapport, rentrer dans l'image, c'est épouser la zébrure transparente, quitter la salle et s'abstraire de la conscience de soi du spectateur symbolisée par l'opacité du rideau.

Le second plan qui entretient *a posteriori* un rapport de rime visuelle avec le photogramme représente une bobine de film posée sur une table que le projectionniste saisit d'une main et extrait de la boîte métallique qui la comprend. La tranche de la bande de celluloïd enroulée autour de son axe produit l'effet d'un disque noir sur lequel se reflète la lumière ambiante de la cabine de projection. Si le film, en tant que support, est ici présenté dans sa matérialité, c'est-à-dire, dans son opacité, le reflet annonce pourtant la transparence de la projection à venir.

Le point commun entre ces deux plans réside dans l'association qui est faite entre la lumière et la monstration du dispositif cinématographique, c'est-à-dire respectivement entre la croyance − la transparence − et la distance − l'opacité −. Encore faut-il noter qu'il ne s'agit pas d'un lien substitutif, mais d'un rapport dialectique : en présentant un caméraman sur le point de se fondre dans la blancheur d'un écran, en filmant le jeu des reflets de la lumière sur une bobine de film sombre, Vertov n'opère pas simplement le passage de l'opacité à la transparence, mais érige en principe stylistique la concomitance de l'une et de l'autre. Le réalisateur définit un paradigme ambivalent, celui d'une position d'une position spectatorielle intermédiaire entre les pôles de la distance et de la croyance.

En d'autres termes, ce que nous lie à l'image, ce n'est pas seulement la naissance du cinéma et le triomphe d'un monde transparent en lequel le spectateur place sa croyance ; c'est aussi la prégnance d'un écran opaque confinant le public dans un rapport distancié. Vertov définit une posture dans laquelle le spectateur n'est pas sommé de trancher entre la croyance et la distance puisque le film maintient la ligne de

prelude to projection. The cameraman breaks free of the limit which separates the theater from the filmic world in order to incorporate himself into the white surface, in the depth of a world in which the spectator places his belief. Under the terms of this relationship, to enter into the image once again is to espouse the transparent zebra pattern, to leave the theater and abstract onself from the consciousness of self of the spectator symbolized by the opacity of the curtain.

The second shot which supports *a posteriori* the relationship of a visual rhyme with the frame in question shows a reel of film placed on a table which the projectionist grabs and extracts from the metal box which contains it. The section of the strip of celluloid wound around its axis produces the effect of a black disk on which the ambient light of the projection booth is reflected. If the film, as support, is here presented in its materiality, that is to say, in its opacity, the reflection, however, prefigures the transparency of the projection to come.

The point of commonality between these two shots resides in the associaiton which is made between light and the display of the film strip, that is to say, respectively between belief—transparency—and distance—opacity. Still, one must note that it's not a matter of a connection of substitution, but a dialectical relationship: in presenting a cameraman on the point of dissolving into the whiteness of a screen, in filming the play of light reflections on a dark reel of film, Vertov brings about not only the passage from opacity to transparency, but establishes as a stylistic principle the concomitance of the one with the other. The director defines an ambivalent paradigm, that of a spectatorial position intermediate between the poles of distance and belief.

In other words, what ties us to the image, is not only the birth of the cinema and the triumph of a transparent world in which the spectator places his belief; it is as well the state of gestation of a dark screen confining the audience within a distanced relationship. Vertov defines a position in which the spectator is not called upon to make a clear contrast between belief and distance since the film maintains the divide

partage entre les deux termes d'une dialectique indécidable : je n'ai pas à choisir entre la présentation transparente du monde et sa *re-présentation* opaque puisque le spectacle du dispositif, précisément, participe de ma croyance. En ce sens, l'épistémologie devient « magique »[2]. Je ne formule, moi, spectateur, un acte de foi en l'image que parce que, d'une certaine façon, je suis capable d'assumer le spectacle même du dispositif. J'ai beau voir l'homme et sa caméra littéralement rentrer dans l'écran de cinéma ceint par les pans du rideau sombre, j'élabore un type de croyance qui consiste déjà à « sortir du cinéma »[3]. Dans ce photogramme, Vertov forge donc une oxymore plastique : en moi se joignent les deux versants d'une indécidable ligne de crête entre la transparence et l'opacité.

1. Cette propension à produire de la lumière à partir de l'obscurité semble annoncer la façon dont Pierre Soulages peint ses toiles abstraites labourées de sillages noirs réfléchissant la lumière naturelle et dont la densité varie en fonction des déplacements du spectateur.
2. Sur les rapports entre magie et épistémologie dans *L'Homme à la caméra*, voir Annette Michelson, « *L'homme à la caméra* : de la Magie à l'Epistémologie », in Dominique Noguez (ed.), Cinéma, théories, lectures, Paris, Klincksieck, 1973, pp. 295-310 (traduction par G. Dupouy).
3. Sur la question de la croyance du spectateur doublée de la conscience du dispositif, on peut se reporter à Roland Barthes : « En sortant du cinéma », Paris, Communication n°23.

between the two terms of an undecidable dialectic: I cannot choose between the transparent presentation of a world and its opaque *re-presentation* since the spectacle of the filmstrip, precisely, participates in my belief. In this sense, epistemology becomes "magic."[2] I, the spectator, do not formulate an act of faith in the image because, in a certain way, I am capable of assuming the spectacle even of the filmstrip. In vain I watch the man and his camera literally return to the screen of the theater enclosed by the two panels of the dark curtain, I elaborate a type of belief which consists already of "leaving the movie theater."[3] In this frame, then, Vertov forges a plastic oxymoron: in me are joined the two slopes of an undecidable watershed between transparency and opacity.

---

1. This propensity to produce light from darkness seems to prefigure the manner in which Pierre Soulages painted his abstract canvasses, plowed with black furrows reflecting natural light and the density of which varies as a function of the distance of the spectator.
2. On the relationship between magic and epistemology in *Man with a Movie Camera*, see Annette Michelson, "*L'homme à la caméra* : de la Magie à l'Epistémologie" ["*Man with a Movie Camera:* from Magic to Epistemology"], in Dominique Noguez (ed.), Cinéma, théories, lectures , Paris, Klincksieck, 1973, pp. 295-310 (translation by G. Dupouy). [Originally "From Magician to Epistemologist: Vertov's *The Man with a Movie Camera,*" in Artforum 10 (1972) : 60-72.].
3. On the question of the belief of the spectator doubled by the consciousness of the filmstrip, one may refer to Roland Barthes « En sortant du cinéma », [*Upon Leaving the Movie Theater*], Paris, Communication n°23. [Reprinted in Theresa Hak Kyung Cha (ed.), Apparatus, New York, 1980.]

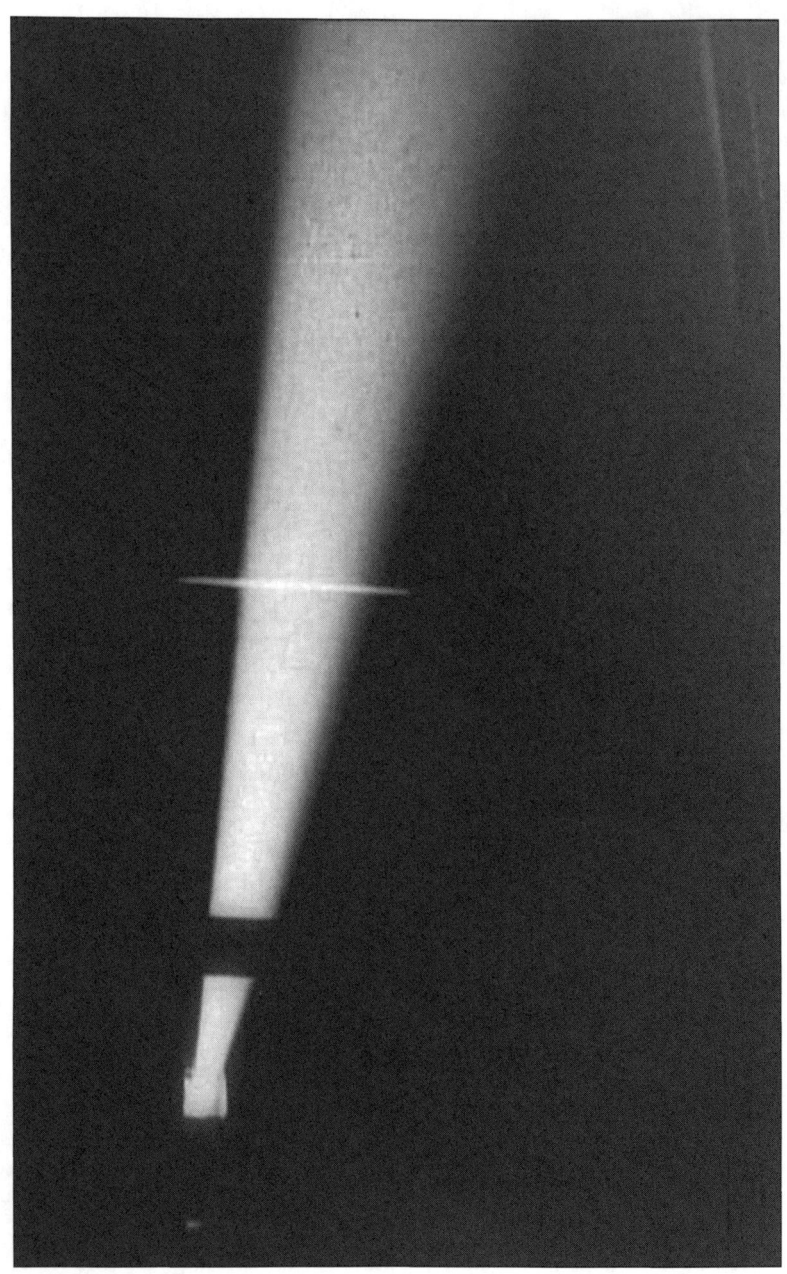

FOUR LEGENDS FOR DZIGA

Abigail Child

1.

Flag waving
Making (relic)
Boxes
Both pedantic and luscious
Divided
In triplicate
Where spring bobbins
BOB
Eager
humorous
And self reflective
Heroic
(hectic) spool

2.

Contemporary to Ives and a younger Cowell, Vertov's earliest experiments in sound remain a driving force behind his pictorial montage. The machine sings, shots are chords or notes, themes recur, the end will see a heraldic recapturing of tunes struck (images seen). Here the proletarian future is idealized through skilled montage—a dance of forks and folk tunes. A utopian combine of intervals: feet and bottles, faces and kitchenware. Culminating in an audience watching an animated camera 'baptized' or drawn out through a mug, filtrated from its load of liquor.

Audience Camera Audience Camera Audience Audience Camera Audience Camera Audience Case of Camera Audience All smiles. A specific blonde [we haven't seen before] raises her eyes in surprise, reminding us of the child in the earlier scene with the Chinese magician. There the young girl shivers with a premature self consciousness; here, the woman is adult, her look quizzical, self-possessed. She raises eyebrows, smiles, and is met with abstraction: a vaguely electronic, watery radio signal. Similar to the magician's act, the insert remains mysterious.

When I first saw *Man With A Movie Camera*, I thought this abstraction possibly a close-up of water from the hydro-electric dam that appears earlier in the film, all artificial curves and slippery surface. I thought too of optical track, and the arrows of metal coming together at the film's head to catapult movie onto screen.

Metonymic of camera and spool, the abstraction plays as techne of the reel. The image —whether water or reel of wire (as the dvd's narrator claims)—signals electricity, referencing wire and wireless power, an origin for "radio ears." The frame is filled with whirring light. The movie cuts from full-frame image to wide shot, three bands of light glisten on the surface in a theater filled with Vertov's audience, transfixed towards this flagrantly odd composite shot. The image reads as an electrocardiogram of film— electric heart, beat, pulse—

as if machine had come alive, become Subject, which indeed it is in this movie. The shot shimmers. It ends the prior montage of cutesy animations to conclude this section.

3.

In this legend, the abstract image is architecture: it makes a corner. It creates a chapter, suggesting conclusion. The image is punctuation, a structural moment in the composition, the end of the section, leading to epilogue.

These two shots, the abstract close-up and its composite, mirror the beginning of the film where projector comes into contact, starts. But here, the image no longer references the apparatus we are about to watch as much as the origins of electric power which initiate and contain the future—heralding energy, movement, modernity (consumerism?).

4.

Not insignificantly, the radio ear starts from inside the Worker's Club. In this sense, the abstract image is the proletariat speaking. The image is the signal for a future which envisions democratic access. It re-reads theatre so film is the future. The sound of wire, static, electronic noise a prelude to sound film, enacting Vertov's wish to make eye touch ear, a literalization of his symphony. The theatre sets the stage with the proletariat at head of machine—mutually, player and spectator. The "mystery" image, then, a referencing of power, short wave, sound echo, access and movie projection in one.

The image an abstraction in a film relentlessly quotidian accords a discussion of propaganda: I am suggesting a menace in the infrastructure.

Electricity meets the entranced audience. Electricity enters, creates radio theater, a "dream theater" where life comes re-processed into the present. The film elevates power to machine, creates a false felicitousness: a unity of worker and her tool. While inside, crowds in theatre watch themselves: a certain edifice of conformity and narcissized enthusiasm, even infantilization in their faces.

As much as the abstraction is unidentifiable, it sources an unnameable, is not 'on line' for the audience. Is un available. Propaganda exists under and around, inside this image.

Even as Mikhail Kauffman rides his motorcycle into the audience, energized and optimistic, we re-read his act from a new century, and find glorification of the machine a problematic song. Even if we acknowledge language as a primary creative abstraction achieved by our species, the twentieth and now the twenty-first centuries record frightening consequences and potential destruction through mechanics of distance.

But this is later. In the movie, the audience is less hypnotized than amazed, less narcotic than entertained. The abstraction, inexplicable or nearly so, becomes by its emptiness, a dream screen, a thrilling punctum and precondition for ambiguous closure.

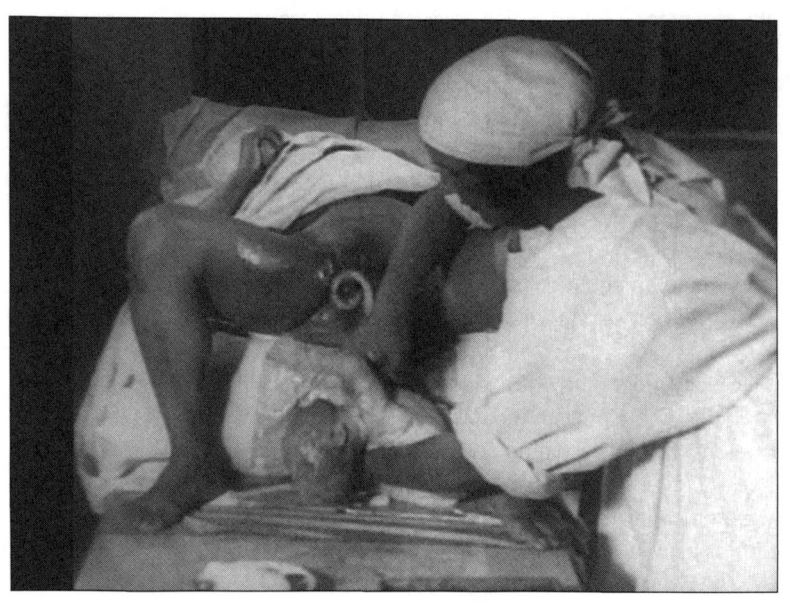

L'ORIGINE DU MONDE

Edwin Carels

Reflecting upon this mysterious image, one wonders what the original audience thought it was seeing, back in 1929. The strange, seemingly abstract shot is preceded by an object animation-sequence about a camera, intercut with close ups of attentive, amused viewers. Following the mysterious shot we get to see a total view of the film auditorium with the same image still on the screen. The reaction shots of the public in the theatre are obviously taken from another context. This sequence actually constitutes some of the least typical editing in the whole film. As if Vertov suddenly gave away to Kuleshov and his experiments with artificially imposed interpretations. Maybe Vertov realised that he needed a trick like this to get away with such a blatant abstraction. Or did he really hope that by that moment in the film, the real audience would enjoy his non-dogmatic, experimental evocation of daily life in the same enthusiastic way as this pro-filmic public? That they would welcome his film as a temporary autonomous zone where freedom of thought and association is stimulated, rather than manipulated?

Obviously, there is no way we can watch this passage with the same curiosity and excitement as Vertov's contemporaries, as if from behind their backs. A first, well-informed guess about the identity of the mysterious image could be that we are seeing a close up of an old 78 rpm record in motion. We know that Vertov conceived his film as a visual symphony (in the same vein as *Symphonie der Grosstadt* by Walther Ruttmann, 1927) and that he had specific ideas about the score to accompany his film. We also know that from his childhood, Vertov developped a keen interest in music, that he studied piano and violin. In 1916-1917, whilst studying medicine at the Psychoneurological

Institute in St. Petersburg, he experimented with "sound collages" in his free time. For his studies of human perception, he recorded and edited natural sounds in his 'Laboratory of Hearing,' trying to create new forms of sound effects by means of the rhythmic grouping of phonetic units. It is in the same period that Denis Arkadievich Kaufman changed his identity to Dziga Vertov, a much more suggestive name, with connotations of "turning, revolving" and thus also of "dynamic thought processess" as opposed to fixed ideas.

But when indeed we watch this filmstill as we should, as a moving image, then it instantly becomes clear that this this cannot be a close up of a record. Yet, it might still be the raw material that we are seeing, one step in the transformation of hard rubber or shellac (this is still the previnyl era) into a music record. If Vertov visually deconstructs so many aspects of his profession and of industrial production in general, then why would he not do the same with his soundtrack? In the beginning of the film we see a live orchestra in the auditorium, only to see it replaced by a mechanical music source at the end of the film, so it seems. After all, the whole film is a celebration of man-machine symbiosis. For his next production, *Enthuziasm* (or *Symphony of the Donbass)*, Vertov finally had the technology available to effectively splice sound and image together, to make one of the most inventive, daring sound films of the first decades.

The virtuoso play with rhythmic editing and the many suggestive images of instruments and sound sources have made *The Man with the Movie Camera* one of the most popular films to compose new scores for (ranging from, to cite just some of the more recent examples, Michael Nyman and Pierre Henry to the Cinematic Orchestra and In the Nursery.) Not that the film actually needs any acoustic support, quite the contrary. The dense, kaleidoscopic imagery can best be responded to as a piece of visual music or in the case of our mysterious image, of purely abstract cinema. The visual equivalent of a few slow notes on a cello, before the climactic last five minutes of film.

The image of an elegantly rotating, shiny black mass can also be read as cryptic signature. Another motif throughout the film, and not entirely different from those images denoting sound, is the variation on circular movement : revolving doors, spinning machines, the turning of the handle of the camera etc. This iconography of the 'swirl' also returns as the finale of the film, in the way that the iris of the camera closes and at the same time fuses with the eye of the cameraman. And it surfaces in the images of the film rolls, as we see them being handled by the director's wife and most loyal contributor Elisaveta Svilova, earlier on in the film. Much less cited than her contemporary Esfir Shub, Elisaveta Svilova deserves just as much recognition as one of the true pioneers of the essayistic editing style. (In most books on filmhistory, she hardly gets a mention or two. Only Annette Michelson dedicated her book to both Svilova and Vertov, and spent extra attention to her in an extended footnote.[1])

Behind the man with the movie camera, indeed there stood the woman with the scissors. As the film is actually more notorious for its editing than for its camerawork, it is a pity that this is not reflected in the title: the woman in the editing room, for instance. In the film Elisaveta Svilova is featured nearly as prominently as the acting cameraman, Vertov's brother Michail Kaufman. But while he appears in the broad daylight, she works isolated in a sombre cell, where she heroically puts the eccentric montage ideas of her man into practice. A labor of love, no doubt, and perhaps a working relationship so intense that it didn't leave any opportunity or energy to raise their own kids. The first time Elisaveta Svilova is introduced in the film, she is sorting out footage of young children. The first time we see her using the scissors, it is to cut a film fragment of a new born baby. Clearly a symbolic choice, but also in tune with the film's ambition to alternate youth and old age, wedding and divorce, scenes of birth and funerals. To my knowledge, *The Man with the Movie Camera* is probably the first non-scientific film to show a mother and child, still connected by the umbilical cord. This spiralling, pulsating, existential link marks the true primal scene of this visionary film.

The composition with the legs wide open in Vertov's version of *L'Origine du Monde* is even accentuated by the preceding and following shot, both also suggesting a "splitting open" of a symmetrical composition. This is "Birth of a Nation" – soviet style. This type of image that, outside of medical films and experimental cinema, has remained taboo for so many decades is not used here to shock or provoke. It accentuates the idea of a new life, a new type of citizen born under a totally new regime. It embodies the constructivist spirit, so strongly felt throughout the film, that soviet men and women are all actively contributing to the creation of a new society. Only now that, in a very different way, in western society people feel that they too can construct 'life' according to their own desires (plastic surgery, artificial insemination, DNA-manipulation) there is no longer a taboo on the realistic imagery of umbilical cords and smear. Remember the 1991 'New Born Baby' Benneton-campaign? One cannot help and wonder whether that baby, born in 1928 during the shooting of the *Man with a Movie Camera*, has lived to see this global campaign reach his or her own native town.

1. *Kino Eye, the Writings of Dziga Vertov*, edited and with an introduction by Annette Michelson, translated by Kevin O'Brien, University of California Press, 1984, page 12.

WORLD OF NAKED TRUTH

François Bucher

Facing an abstract still you are immediately turned to the silence of cinema. More so, you are turned to the task of thinking the image in its degree zero. A still from a film within a film, framed in a movie theater within another movie theater, about a man with a movie camera mounting his tripod on quickening trains and cars; a man shooting the machine, not the star, magically transmitting his live images to a live audience in a filmed theater, seen by another audience, now in another century. The cacophony escalates until this abstract still. Cut.

I want to deform the phrase at the top of Mount Carmel in Saint John of the cross' diagram: Up here there is no figure because the imageless image is to itself its own figure.

1929. *The Man with a Movie Camera*. My father was born in 1929. He was born to the eternal exile of a region of shifting identities—Alsace; a boy under German occupation, in the core of an entrenched, resistance family, wounded, deep in the heart by an unshakeable Germanic romanticism. This meant that thought had an opportunity to prosper in him. Where the stable subject is dissolved, where there is no point of arrival, because the very conditions of existence within the boundaries of history are what have to come into question, incessantly, there thought may silently take place. A point of arrival is what a classical narrative offers us. Exile is the suspension (of the suspension), the underground, resistance movement; an explosion of the line that takes us from here to there. In a certain sense, thought is always and necessarily in exile. Deleuze speaks about audio-vision in this way: "at the same time that this word rises in the air, that which it is talking to us about buries itself underground"[1] Between the air where it rises and the underground were it advances stealthily, there is an impossible place, a place where we cannot dwell, where we cannot spend the night. That is then the thought on exile that concerns us. Vertov is determined to kidnap the image from the spell of narrative power; to suspend it, in the endless suspension that calls us to think... that we call *thinking*. This endless suspension is what Cinema and Philosophy share: they can only speak paradoxically, their language needs to speak about itself, they have a genetic "incurable speech defect"[2]; a gag, Agamben points out, in the sense of "something that could be put in your mouth to hinder speech as well as in the sense of the actor's improvisation meant to compensate a loss of memory or an inability to speak"[3]. "Not being able to figure something out in language"[4] and yet presenting this impossibility: a radio eye, a voluntary knee jerk, an involuntary determination. Vertov resists the movie that placates us in a dream of stars and lipstick. Confronted with this he sees the salvation of the machine that produces the communist imagination[5]. He wants to sink his fingers into the matter of the machine that presents movement; to puncture the celluloid at every corner, so that we might jump into the void as it is about to envelop us in the amnesia of the spectacle. We have to imagine that jump as a happy one, "Il faut imaginer Sisyphe heureux."

Agamben says that thought is "defined by the very capacity of de-creating the real"[6] (the reel), and memory (which is the matter of cinema as much as cinema is the matter of memory) is that which "makes the unaccomplished accomplished and the accomplished unaccomplished."[7] In this paradox of time, in this "prolonged hesitation between image and sense" of cinema, as Paul Valéry would say, we remain without a ground, without a country, without a homeland to return to, without an Empire to accomplish, inoperative. Yet acting. Vertov sees the machine of cinema as splendid as long as it doesn't make a pact with *mise en scène*; "Vodka, church and cinema, the three methods by which capitalism puts the worker to sleep." And just as Syberberg had said that we have to judge Hitler as a filmmaker (*metteur en scène*), Vertov is anticipating the Hollywood dream in the hands of fascism. Let's not speak just now of what happens with the dream of the machine.

In *The Man with a Movie Camera* Vertov anticipates another dilemma of contemporary culture. In a series of quasi-didactic shots he exposes the difference between the noble activity that leads to *production* and the frivolity of cosmetic *service;* between the factory or the cutting table on one hand and the beauty parlor on the other: "We, the shoemakers of cinema say to you, the shoe shiners, that we do not recognize your seniority in the making of film objects."⁸ Serge Daney points out a similar difference when defining the paradigms of Cinema and Television. In Daney's terms cinema stands for the cultural, artisanal memory, of the tools of production while television is the amnesia of the prefabricated, the cliché. In an article in *Libération* he quotes a term coined by Jean-Claude Biette—"filmed cinema" when he discovers films like *The Big Blue* and *Out of Africa* as pieces made entirely of publicity spots, posing as cinema; films that are not produced, but programmed. Shiny shoes that don't know the first thing about how they came to be shoes but which keep getting more and more layers of wax applied onto them. Which means that advertisement has proceeded to the sampling of a small part that it inherited from cinema, it has created preassembled cinema shreds and reshuffled them in a vacuum. The immobility of this arrested history, according to Daney, finds its epitome in telemarketing, a quasi return of the image, to the pre-cinematic *spotlight* function of the vitrine of the 19th century. The post-publicity film is not just contaminated, through television by advertisement but *fully* defined by advertisement. It is therefore the place of an end, a *cul de sac*: not the immobility of the still but the dead stillness of un-thought.

Taking an airplane from Bogotá, I notice again the motto that so many corporate alliances use. I read the words "one world" again, as I have so many times in so many different variations. Then I sit and watch, in my little monitor, the expensive tracking shots fading into each other, of Japanese gardens, close-up color saturated flowers and high pleasant mountaintops of serene accomplishment. The chosen muzak is a perfect audio-visual match to this relaxing image therapy that I am subjected to. The image does nothing to the sound and the sound does nothing to the image. In the depth of the image there is nothing but another image, so we fade in. I think of this pseudo esthetic moment which hides under each delicate petal its mindless truth: that the image serves the omniscient principle of "social control" and nothing about it reaches anymore towards an ethical horizon. I am a passenger, the only thing to add is maybe that I am an economy class passenger, and I did not pre order a vegetarian dish. All the rest is unimportant. I will behave like all the others, I will be soothed by the flowers and the *new age* music before *take-off*. The image has been *programmed* for that. It has one function: appeasement, the mindless downer that Vertov addressed so emphatically.

Another day. I am flying Lufthansa to Berlin. I see the list of films that I am going to be zapping through, since now I am no longer "in the movies" when flying (as in the 70s and 80s) but in front of my own private monitor and with my own *télé-commande*, to use the more graphic French notion rather than the English—remote control—which applies less in the crowded situation of economy class (it might apply better in first class). I notice that Lufthansa is showing *Wag the Dog*, a film that (I have been told) even Saddam showed to his people to illustrate, through a fiction of the *image-making* apparatus of his enemy, what that very enemy was up to. I pause to analyze the situation, since *Wag the Dog* is not a current film and there is no reason for it to be listed with the current program of Hollywood blockbusters. Daney comes to mind again: the step from the paradigm of *production* to that of *programming*. Lufthansa *reads* the world (it is *one world* after all). Lufthansa knows where I'm coming from and were I'm going to (it's the business of airlines… and the business of television which doesn't place its automobile advertisements in the mornings, nor its toy car commercials late at night for the same reason). It is interesting to think that the movies now are like trump cards. In Hollywood, a producer[9] finds a script that *works* (this *is* where the act of creation now resides). Then he chooses what director can shoot it appropriately, which is an insignificant detail, since out there he can find many with the *know-how*, the *technique* of assembling clichés—what film schools churn by the thousands. Likewise the programmer of Lufthansa chooses amongst stocks of movies according to departure and destination. The programmer knows you are coming from America where two things are being discussed: the 2004 elections and the phony reasons for going to war with Iraq. He programs the film that resonates. *Wag the Dog* is a good choice, it works, it is perfect. As Deleuze says, to criticize television is a matter of addressing its perfection not its imperfection. The perfection of how *Wag the Dog* is slid on my plate, like reheated airplane food makes me think of a sentence of Agamben "The media tyranny wants appalled, but impotent citizens." I am not thinking, I am being entertained by the idea that I think.[10]

Vertov, like his sometime antagonist Eisenstein, posits a cinematographic image that "must have a shock effect on thought and force thought to think itself as much as thinking the whole"[11] Modern history destroys that "whole", succeeding it with an irrational cut, a non-totalizable relation. But this epic quest to create a communist deciphering of reality has to be seen as what it is; an offer of thought. And *The Man with a Movie Camera* is the testament of a heroic act, always read in the present (Kaufman is still filming a speeding locomotive, coming towards him, from its very tracks… for us). Even if in 1929 Vertov can only conceive of a "negative of time", a derivative from the visual equation of movement (as Deleuze would say), he still remains the striking example of a man with a radical agenda that we fully subscribe to today: to push the image to its very limit (to the limit that our condition allows us as *beings-in-language*, in the contingency of historical specificity)… and then beyond.

1. Deleuze, Gilles, "Qu'est-ce que l'acte de création?" *Trafic* Fall 1998. p. 139.
2. Agamben, Giorgio, "Notes on Gesture," in *Means Without End: Notes on Politics*, Minneapolis: University of Minnesota Press, 2000.
3. *ibid.*
4. *ibid.*
5. Benjamin writes that Marx secularizes the notion of a Messianic time in the concept of a classless society.
6. Agamben, Giorgio, "Face au cinema et à l'Histoire, à propos de Jean-Luc Godard," *Le Monde des Livres*, (6 October 1995).
7. Agamben, Giorgio, "Le Cinéma de Guy Debord," *Image et Memoire* (1998).
8. Vertov, Dziga, and Annette Michelson. *Kino-Eye : The Writings of Dziga Vertov*. Berkeley, Ca.: University of California Press, 1984. p 37.
9. Which should really be called "programmer".

10. After writing this I was surprised to feel the astonishing power of *The Battle of Algiers* in April 2004 at the Film Forum in New York. What is the difference then between the mimicry of a historical dialogue that drops dead in the moment when it is presented (the mimicry of thought) and another one that actualizes the vibrations of the past with such vigor? The power of *The Battle of Algiers* resists any context of presentation as much as its characters resisted the occupation. In his years writing for *Libération* Serge Daney was always asking the question of a reception in the *now*, watching a film on television and considering it afresh from the perspective of its new contingency. Regarding *Wag the Dog*, the film itself, I think that it is just one of those complicated operations which do exactly the opposite of what they seem to be doing. They render futile a complex thought on the frighteningly sophisticated and disabling governmental mechanisms of manipulation. They resample the same cliché that the fatuous epithet "conspiracy theory" is already setting forth. They offer a kind of closure for one of the most prevalent collective anxieties; they basically sell a feeling of empowerment to a powerless public: *we are in the know*—they tell us. The programming of *Wag the Dog* by Lufthansa is like the preassembly of a preassembly, the resampling of resampled material, absolutely unfertile, the image of *thought* as entertainment.
11. Deleuze, Gilles, *Cinema 2: The Time-Image*, trans. Hugh Tomlinson and Robert Galeta (London: Athlone Press, 1989), 168.

Diane Bertolo

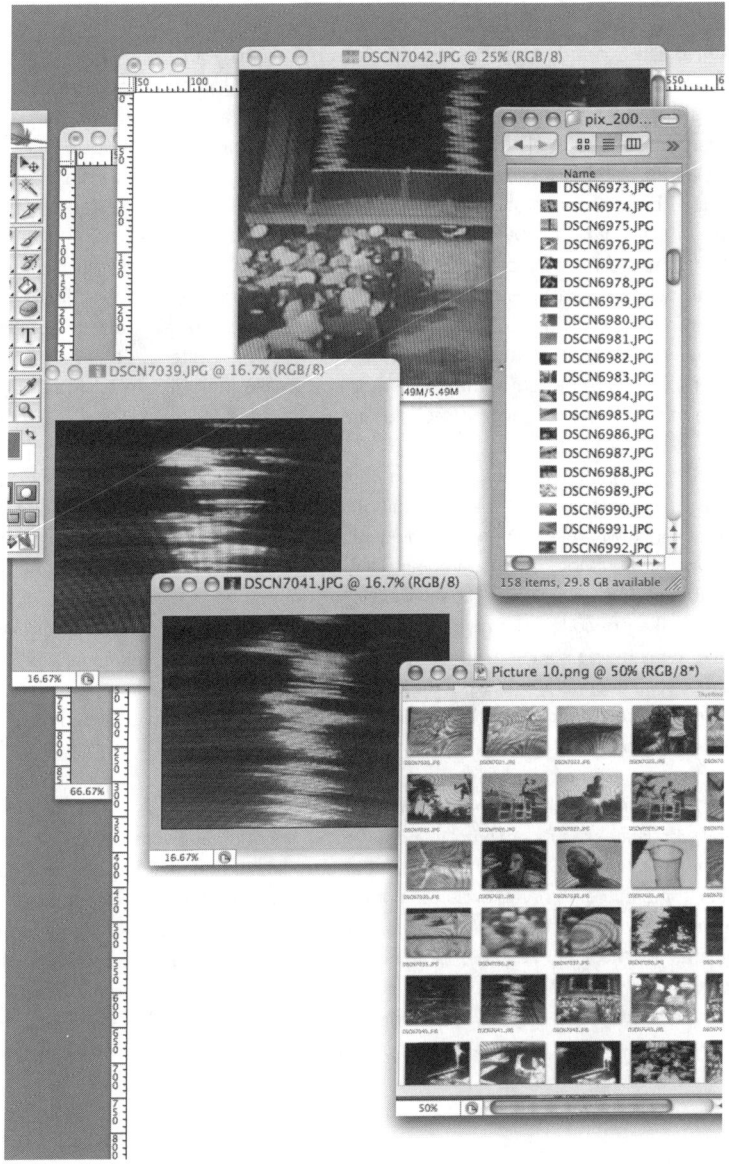

EVERY MAN HIS OWN AURA

Walter Benjamin

HAVING DIED nearly seventy years before receiving your email, I am somewhat at a loss as to how to respond. Nonetheless, I think it important to recognize, even from the grey silence of the dead, that, in spite of my pessimism about the use of film in the creation of revolutionary critique—as long as its dominant models are determined by Southern Californian capitalists—I believe that comrade Vertov did contribute in some measure, at least in *Man with a Movie Camera*, to the questioning of the role of the aura in the new reality of the Soviet Union. Though it bears only indirectly on the still you sent me, and since the dead are strictly prevented from extending their literary output, if you like, you may quote in your collection the passage below from an essay of mine which, in spite of its repeated distortion in recent years, may offer some durable insight into what is at stake in this frame of motion picture film:

> The film responds to the shriveling of the aura with an artificial build-up of the "personality" outside the studio. The cult of the movie star, fostered by the money of the film industry, preserves not the unique aura of the person but the "spell of the personality," the phony spell of a commodity. So long as the movie-makers' capital sets the fashion, as a rule no other revolutionary merit can be accredited to today's film than the promotion of a revolutionary criticism of traditional concepts of art. We do not deny that in some cases today's films can also promote revolutionary criticism of social conditions, even of the distribution of property. However, our present study is no more specifically concerned with this than is the film production of Western Europe.
>
> It is inherent in the technique of the film as well as that of sports that everybody who witnesses its accomplishments is somewhat of an expert. This is obvious to anyone listening to a group of newspaper boys leaning on their bicycles and discussing the outcome of a bicycle race. It is not for nothing that newspaper publishers arrange races for their delivery boys. These arouse great interest among the participants, for the victor has an opportunity to rise from delivery boy to professional racer. Similarly, the newsreel offers everyone the opportunity to rise from passer-by to movie extra. In this way any man might even find himself part of a work of art, as witness Vertov's *Three Songs About Lenin* or Iven's *Borinage*. Any man today can lay claim to being filmed.

Ericka Beckman

Stick figure 04: exposure 2 seconds, Polaroid slide film.

Yann Beauvais

Un photogramme prélevé de *L'homme à la caméra* et c'est tout le cinéma qui surgit.

Le cinéma, justement ; pas le divertissement.

C'est un usage du cinéma dont nous avons toujours grandement besoin.

Se perdre à partir de cette image capturée : le photogramme comme fil d'Ariane.

À la réception du mail, je décidais de ne pas revoir une fois encore, *L'homme à la caméra* mais, de me laisser emporter autant par les souvenirs, que par des pensées éparses, dynamisées par ce photogramme gelé.

Une image en somme : *a still* ; en anglais : *still life*, quasiment une nature morte. En tout cas un mouvement figé ; ne devrait-on pas dire dans ce cas : suspendu comme le serait la vie qui ne tient qu'à un souffle. Cet état particulier de l'image arrêtée, met en péril le film quant à son défilement. Il suspend son vol, son flot. Il s'abîme pour devenir nature morte. Le cinéma s'éteint dans le photogramme figé : la photo de film. La lumière n'est plus transportée, prête à être codé de diverses manières, comme celle qui consiste à narrer d'innombrables récits.

Le cinéma éteint dans le photogramme gelé évoque d'autres situations, d'autres récits tel celui qui célèbre la disparition de Lénine et dans ce cas, la mort est montrée, pas la nature ; la mort. Nature morte, ça sonne toujours étrange si on pense à Dziga Vertov. En effet il y va plus de la célébration de l'homme moderne, de celui qui fait corps avec la machine, qui domestique les forces machiniques et travaille dynamiquement la nature. On ne peut pas dire que la nature soit chez Dziga Vertov un espace bucolique, elle est avant tout productive, au service de l'homme, du plan (à comprendre dans tous les sens), afin

Yann Beauvais

A single frame is taken from *The Man with a Movie Camera* and the entire cinema rises into view.

Precisely, the cinema, not entertainment.

It's a use of the cinema of which we are still in such great need.

To lose oneself by means of this captured image; the frame as Ariadne's thread.

When I got the email, I decided not to look at *The Man with a Movie Camera* once again, but to allow myself to be carried away by memories, as much as by scattered thoughts, energized by this frozen frame.

An image, to sum up: *a still*; in English: *still life*, almost a still life. In any case, a fixed movement; shouldn't one say in this case: suspended, as would be a life that hangs upon a breath. This particular state of the arrested image, brings the film into danger as far as its unraveling[1] is concerned. It suspends its flight, its torrential flow. It collapses to become a still life. The cinema is extinguished in the fixed frame: the photograph of film. Light is no longer transported, read to be coded in various ways, like one that consists of narrating innumerable stories.

The cinema extinguished in the frozen frame evokes other situations, other stories, like the one that celebrates the loss of Lenin and in this case, death is shown, not nature—but death. Still life, it still sounds strange, if you think about Dziga Vertov. In fact, there is no more celebration of modern man, of one who joins bodies with the machine, who domesticates mechanical forces and works nature dynamically. You cannot say that for Dziga Vertov nature is a bucolic space, it is above all productive, in the service of man, of the plan (to be understood in all senses),[2] in order that he may unfold new horizons. Let's imagine that

qu'il puisse déployer de nouveaux horizons. Imaginons qu'en fonction du sens de lecture de ce photogramme envoyé, la nature de la chose représentée s'offre le luxe de se transmuter.

Si on respecte l'envoi, on voit un instantané dans le déversement d'un rouleau de câble, la vitesse créant cette zébrure réfléchissant la lumière. Par contre si l'on se saisit de l'image horizontalement c'est-à-dire irrévérencieusement, alors c'est la courbure d'un cours d'eau, cours d'eau domestiqué afin de produire de l'électricité. Dans les deux cas, la nature de l'image s'égare dans la contradiction qu'elle dévoile, à savoir nous montrer du mouvement au travers du figé. On finirait par penser que cette image-même est alors un parangon du cinéma lui-même, qui produit le mouvement à coûts trop tirés.

Les zébrures, ne devrait-on les envisager comme des striures, produisent la transformation ; elles sont les agents qui inscrivent à même leurs irrégularités l'incroyable vitesse de défilement de ce câble, ou de ces flots qui ne veulent pas arrêter leurs cours. Ces irrégularités me font penser aux *doodles (scribbles)* de Len Lye, qui sont selon sa terminologie les signes énergétiques de notre cerveau, avant qu'ils ne soient codés et qu'il a transposé dans quelques-uns de ses films au moyen du grattage constituant par la même une énergétique cinématographique démontée, c'est-à-dire qui ne fait pas appel au montage, mais au traces de lumière sur le support même.

Mais voilà que cette image s'égare, nous conduisant vers d'autres horizons. Ça commençait pourtant bien et puis avec cet arrêt de l'image, la pensée prend le relais, et commence à dériver. Comme si l'image présentée par-delà sa familiarité, ne pouvait se suffire. Comme si elle renvoyait systématiquement à d'autre(s). En transit sur nos écrans, dans notre tête, sur le livre, au détour d'une page, elle ne fait que passer, mais elle en appelle d'autres, et d'autres encore.

Elle ne transporte plus la lumière, mais renvoie à une autre circulation de l'information, qui veut qu'il ne saurait y avoir juste une image.

Une image, en l'occurrence une photo c'est déjà un film arrêté comme

as a function of the sense of the reading of this frame, which was sent out, the nature of the thing represented allows itself the luxury of transmutation.

If one respects what was sent, one sees a snapshot of the discharge of a reel of cable, speed creating these zebra-stripe reflections of light. On the other hand, if one apprehends the image horizontally, that is, irreverently, then it's the arc of a stream of water, a stream of water domesticated to produce electricity. In both cases, the nature of the image gets lost in the contradiction it unveils, that is, showing movement through what is fixed. One ends up thinking that this very image is, then, a paradigm of the cinema itself, which produces movement at over-extended costs.[3]

The zebra-stripes—shouldn't one imagine them as striations—produce the transformation; they are agents which inscribe, in their very irregularities, the incredible speed of passage of this cable, or of these torrents, which refuse to arrest their course. These irregularities make me think of *doodles (scribbles)* by Len Lye, which are, in his terminology, the energetic signs of our brains before they are encoded and which he transposed in some of his films by means of scratching, constituting through this a dismantled cinematic energetics, that is, one which makes no appeal to editing, but to traces of light on the filmstrip itself.

But here, this image wanders off, leading us toward other horizons. It started off well enough, but then with this arrest of the image, thought makes a fresh start, and begins to drift. As if the image presented outside its familiar terms was not enough. As if it systematically referred back to another or to others. In transit on our screens, in our heads, in the book, at the turning over of a page, it only passes by, but it calls forth others, and others still.

It no longer transports light, but returns to another circulation of information, that would recognize more there than just an image.

An image, in this case, a photograph, is already an arrested film as Hollis Frampton said. The image of this man with a movie camera can-

l'a dit Hollis Frampton. L'image de cet homme à la caméra ne saurait se maintenir dans une solitude qui ne participe ni de l'image, ni du film, celui-ci autant que tous les autres. Malgré son arrêt, la prolifération n'est pas potentiellement éteinte. L'image comme pivot générateur de renvois infinis. Cette circulation est sans doute ce qui nous préoccupe le plus quand on fait des images en mouvement : générer des proliférations et des lignes de fuite, déplacer les frontières.

Se pose alors la question du choix de cette image comme prétexte à la glose, mais direz-vous un rouleau de câble n'est pas si éloigné d'un écheveau quelconque, d'où la nécessité par conséquent de rendre hommage à quelque alchimiste inconnu qui hanterait le cinéma autant que le communisme c'est-à-dire comme l'aurait dit Lénine : le socialisme + l'électricité. Ainsi l'électricité au cœur du dispositif d'un pays en construction se trouve être à la fois le courant qui permet de rendre compte de l'électrification du pays et par conséquent indirectement de rendre compte par le cinéma de l'avancée du projet, qui lui-même est un défilement alterné d'un courant d'image figé. La bobine autant que le rouleau peuvent se dérouler jusqu'à se figer dans une image archétypale qui les convoque ainsi à nouveau selon d'autres débits, qui ne tiennent bien souvent qu'à un calibrage de 0 et 1.

Donc une image.

not maintain itself in a solitude which participates neither in the image, nor in film, the latter as much as any of the others. In spite of its arrested state, proliferation is not potentially brought to an end. The image as an axis, generating infinite reverberations. This circulation is no doubt what preoccupies us most when we make moving images: to generate proliferations and lines of flight,[4] to displace the frontiers.

The question then comes to be posed of the choice of this image as the pretext for a gloss, but a reel of cable is not so distant from a skein of any sort, from which, the consequent necessity of rendering homage to some unknown alchemist, who would seem to haunt the cinema as much as communism, that is, as Lenin would have said: socialism + electricity. Thus, electricity—at the heart of the apparatus of a country under construction—may be discovered to be, at one and the same time, the current which permits the recognition of the electrification of the country and, as a result, of the indirect recognition by means of the cinema of the advance of the project, which, is itself an alternating procession of a flow of fixed images. A film reel as much as a spool of wire can unreel to the point of fixing itself in an archetypal image, which thus summons them once again according to other outputs of current, which have to do quite often only with a calibration based on 0's and 1's.

An image, then.

1. A play on words suggesting both the capacity of the film to resist interpretation and its transit on the screen.
2. Here an untranslatable pun on "plan," which in French means, among other things: "Plan" as in a Five Year Plan, "plan" as in a map or diagram, and "shot" as in a film.
3. Here, an untranslatable allusion to Duchamp's *Anémic Cinéma*. Beauvais writes "a coûts trop tirés," an echo of Duchamp's "Inceste ou passion de famille, à coups trop tirés."
4. Here, "lignes de fuite," literally lines of flight. An allusion is made to Deleuzian "lines of flight." Lost in translation is the original idiomatic sense of perspective projections on which both Deleuze and Beauvais play.

CONSTRUCTIVISM MYSTERY

Bruce Andrews

1.

    Future....

Words on that "film without words," *The Man with a Movie Camera.*

Writing around & about *"absolute writing in film"*

Simpler futuro-

Covert sensing

White graze, the means unentrapped

    Singularized time....

Reading the single frame — shaved down to bits

Cellular torpedo

Point singes

Momentary conquests

Shotput night

Engaging the point in pointillism

Accept the dose — motion slowed, frozen, deanimated

Durationally it gets an incomplete

Dislumbering punctuaters
The tempo has been taken away, the visual changes interrupted

Abstract....

Every document is fractional

Differential shadow, take the tights off

Each — "a separate little document"

Each — of the "signifying pieces"

A unit in some architecture — noiselessly

Title-less, declassé

How close to a pure optical beat?

Stroboscopic pulsation — an essentialism

Thank you for "lacking metaphorical implications"

Shine (built in) from urgent agitational abstraction

Semiabstract, just fine for a transition

Beyond the superficial polish of "the shoeshiners"

The single moment makes itself perfectible, imaginatively

Clean your glasses

Do you have an absolute reading ready?

In relation to....

How, then What

Wrong? — in relation to truth
Species/specious Pravda

The shot doesn't reveal its own technique, does it?

Nor its identity as anything but... "kinoks" of the brain

Comper fête [sic?]

Pre-sense....

A basis for constructing with intervals

Bubbly preliminaries of making sense — incessantly

Post-idiot

Confectionary confetti

Semantics on the run

Motives....

'Unmotivated mischief,' or mischief because unmotivated. OK, so the entirety of the matter rests upon a single question: what is motivation?

Motivation — establishing a [definable] relationship: to an outside social context, to an inwardly-settled personal psychology, or to orders positioned purely inside the test. Let's define it!

Confusion antidote

Anti-mystification

A fantasy of order

"The poetry of unheard numbers..."

2.

    Transparency....

Oversight provided

You kino-see dear too clear

As if you just engage in *deducing* from the material

Bubblepop up the 'radium extraction' (Mayakovsky)

Soak up the schematizing

Sight, a dismount

Footage — to attempt generalization, constructed visually

Tele-eye refrains from comment

Your eye still crawls around

Face the facts, the *"zhizneenny fakty"* ("life-facts") — with *"the enthusiasm of fact*s"

A transparent visible world without your assault

Not stylized, or dressed up: you undress event

Fist o' facts, "lightning flashes of facts"

Almost furious today

The feral eyeball

Imposter ebbs, fuzzy film-fact

Emetic vs. mimetic

Illusionism skewered

The real & the tangible via encrustation

Junk crisper

(Actual sound of the ...?)

    Moment....

Continuity keeps you at arm's length

Separated from any (usually it would be narrative) continuity, materials start to present themselves 'at close range'

Intimacy joins up with discontinuity

Faster prototype, one of several zaum-like 'verbal flashes'

Itsy

Likened to a Mayakovskian one word to a verse line intensification, or to Osip Brik's 'Rhythmicosyntactic Theory'

Are we close enough to the seeming real, the facts, the 'it is' — to fetishize?

Fantasy taint

Momentary circumferential bruising

"Reduced to a small rectangle within the real screen, the moving image on the screen-within-the-screen looks like the theater's 'window' facing reality; although it is not always possible to identify what is projected on the screen-within-the-screen (e.g., the ambiguous shot associated with the rotating spool of wire, whirling strips of light, or spinning cones on wheels)...": Vlada Petric, *Constructivism in Film*, p. 111

Enigma....

Your obsession with quasi-verisimilitude blurs

A flamboyance (at least, if not a hypertrophy) of montage — even to the presentation of a single *interpretable frame* — will resist the project of straightforward representation

Thicken flub

What if: indistinct

"the famous 'enigmatic shot,' composed of rotating horizontal and curved lines that form zigzag patterns projected on the screen-within-the-screen; it is impossible to figure out the representational signification of this shot even after repeated screenings. Only when examined frame by frame does it become clear that the
photographed object is a rotating spool of wire.": Petric, p. 136

If the frame had been representationally identifiable with ease, it probably would have been excluded

You face an optical 'transform' of raw material into a graphic abstraction & then into a multi-level self-referring pictorial composite

Autonomy....

Yet once the audience is revealed — in the next shot — any pictorial flatness derived from foregrounding the image is shredded

For now: grooveless clan jitters

Every moment as a seizure

By itself the individual shot sustains some integrity, some immutability — maybe even a surrogate for a referential fix

The still adds a certain inviolability to the situation — making it more of a self-sufficient, autonomous fixture

Jigsaw parts

Means get turned into ends

> *Doubts....*

You're undoubling the data

A crease out of sight

A deredundancy, a perceptual emergency

Corneal flamboyan

Crankier & surreptitious, yiked up

Preach jigsaw slither

A utilitarian trauma

Material pressurized, confusion giftwrapped

Chemical beauts

A motorized groping

Let go

Ungovernable by law

Flange debris

Reality feeds on you

Your "eyes, spinning like propellers, take off into the future"

3.

    In itself....

Facts, the same night

Time's negative — souped-up sexed-up

Colophonics silent, optical pulsensationalist

What if: squeaky

A near-flicker effect, but within the frame itself — without having to cut in 'interfering' black frames

A relentless singular

Prepsychic neural rampage

Text on hammock

The *interval* before & after disappears

A brief tracking shot of itself

You missed it?

An accidental mystery, a dreamy blurry in-between

    Spectacle....

Its devices aren't self-baring

Flamboyance bereavement

Another animated stop-trick — to make the sizzle dazzle

An uncapsize

Frosted pouffing brain in flunk

Buddy of, singsong

Skew me, hon' — mercy cramps

Sleep blink safe-deposit

One moment of "mesmerization" — but not by means of staging

All-sided lure, attraction, "all-around dependence"

Witnessing or rehab

How's your protesting consciousness — circumvented yet?

Can you hear you?

You, props

Are you the intertitle?

>*Disillusion....*

Enigma — a 'making it difficult'

A lack of self-evidence in the device parallels a lack of self-evidence about the thematics

Assertive indecision — especially when a more detailed, pulled back view comes next

Perceptual dipstick probe

En travestie

Daring anti-icon

The single frame only part of the subsequent composite — of the audience in time & the spool in motion

Cinematic illusion undercut on both ends: the puzzle of the image's content & its screen-within-screen positioning, later revealed in a reversal

The smart ones are hard to pin down

Open Self....

Unresolved, off guard but not caught

Not sweet & not an embrace

Kibbitzing over Time being paralyzed (freeze-frame)

You're not getting any camera superimposed on

Rampage for your sizzle

You can't be made to see; "forceful transfer" doesn't always work. It can just as quickly backfire

The live feed threatens to continue

No "capture" — no "solution" — no "expedient"

An anti-contagion, questionably disobliging

Cinematic paramedics

You "I, a machine," you live in the post-unanimous

You are being built; you are building

Nothing fully available to causal or diegetic control

Outward continuity — left abandoned

Self-reference — a pedagogy of differences

An unimpersonating quotient per individual

A self-blueprinting hopped up

Depsychologized as solicitation

Any 'terrible underside of things' becomes inside-out

The timing of montage pulls itself inside-out, "the negative of time" — "a kind of *Communist decoding of reality*"

    Context....

Reading the frame as a frame

CHOICE TEST

Thematic resonance arising mostly from the way bits are organized, the traces are fixed, beyond a single frame into a "film-object"

How socialized the kino-eye gets to become

To binge on grasp — cooler chrysalis

Optically one speed frozen in a moment; sensibly: set in motion by *context*, by *social framing* & *'facework'*

Any semantic wherewithal you bring to this moment helps to "clarify the relations of workers with each other"

A whirlpool of interactions is taken back up inside the frame (as if: back inside the flying saucer)

To hypothesize: some social command transmitted

The scale of the moving inside
Unbend each chance, each sashay

Synthesizing is inside

Frame — to foster a relationship of fit, of appropriateness, of contextual 'sensical'ness on behalf of the concretest facts (particulars)

And "with plus and minus signs"

4.

    Process....

What is moving?

You celebrate movement — miniatures of social change

This "*dynamic geometry* of the shot," this "geometrical extract of movement"

Filigree flamethrower — wieldliness

Irregularity's triumph

Oops lever, feral dashes

An anti-carelessness

A sass of delicacy delicacy got desperate to key in

What's the concrete sensuous force?

Filmmaking process always crowding in on the ghosts of thematic unspooling

Could this be that 'break down' required for training? Or for liberation?

    Readership....

The site of this stationary spot — before the beautification [*grimirovanie*] campaign

Kino-eye gives way for your activity as a reader

Reading as model for what lies beyond consumption (or 'mere consumption')

TASTEST

So proud of — reader as heroic participant

Too pomp, telltale

Reading as a counter-Hallelujahism

You sensory explorer, a bleedthrough ordained

To read, "maneuvering in the [if you're lucky] chaos of movement"

Thanks for the rapid

Spectator crowned the montagist

A high contrast black & white flattening that erases most vestiges of diegetic 'positioning'

Spectatorial shooters-match

Fracas rhetor

Pomp that stuff — unveigled elocutionary

In sequence: shifting angles of observation, with self-reference added on & any clearcut point of view frazzled

> *Production*....

Ongoing cinematic work... the Movement of Construction

An architecture that doesn't preexist, that's built before our eyes

A factory of footage, inchage, a slushier mathematics of fabrication

Fabricate the killjoy

Post-muzak novelty

Effects sluice out perfectible

What game could make this? What embrace could make this? What blows could make this? What accidents could make this?

Reading supreme — Production supreme

    Mechanics....

Less clumpier machinic delight

"The race of points, lines, planes, volumes" — rocket-propelled

Being defibrillated

"Hurrah for the poetry of machines, propelled and driving; the poetry of levers, wheels, and wings of steel; the iron cry of movements"

Electricity's pollen — "electricity's unerring ways"

Steel crackling

Cyborg yet?

Here you have THE NEW PERSON, "*the new man*," with "the light, precise movements of machines"

Music would wag tail

    Interval....

There is no "given instant"

The individual shot works as a "montage phrase"

A montage cadence all by itself

Box within box

Swallows its own transitions whole

THEORY OF INTERVALS

Intervals are *inside* the moment

Does one part of the frame instruct another? — or instruct us in the *use* of another?

The movement of chiaroscuro (oh fuck your spelling) inside the frame

The intervals interiorized

Pseudo parquet

The frame leans on or puts its shadow over the next: composite, with audience

Echo: rotating plates on the editing table

The rotating filmstrip echoing in our mind — makes every such frame fearful of the scissors that precede it & might follow it

Movement inscribed inside the context of another
Can you get where you want to be? — moving between the frames, proportionalizing guesswork?

It's not as if you have to be 'dummied up & lawyered up'

Intervallic crossover: what ideological premonition just occurred?

What are you waiting to be juxtaposed?

This is a rhythmic brand of "agitation with facts," byproducts of the 'Fact Factory'

What's "the internal rhythm"?

Rhythm spatialized — within things moving as if you're indexing a percussive beat (of a word or syllable, say, beyond any syntactical lock-step)

Intervals preexist — Material intervals

Make the stitches big

    Conflict....

A semantic rhythm

A shot which may function as a 'subversive' or thematic antithesis — not only to the sequence surrounding, but to your own e
xpectations & codings

The ideological connections

Shots in exchange — unequal exchange, fair & free trade, or... battling, to spark off kinesthetic energy

Unconscious structured like a yardsale

Blood on sprockethole

Contrary to

Opposites counterposed

Inside the singular: oppositionally organized features

The overdetermined unit, the popular contest node

Colliding dodgems, whirlpoolizing

Verdict fry-off

An accusation of collision

A bullfight with

The thematic connotations are wayward enough to prevent a contradiction: there's no meaning already solidly enough established for an entire sequence to be *contradicted*

You don't need to *resolve* a conflict-juxtaposition

The 'higher math' is in the overtones

5.
        Awakening....

Oneiric blink

Faktura

Constructivist in the mirror crowning a sizzle

To what do you owe the pressure?

Pixilatté

Flickering — to have just dreamed, a slow decelerando

Stand-off

Unbewitching

Lit fuse

Subtext: impatience

A revolt against kinetic (or kinesthetic) resolution

An image on the verge of being miniaturized, compressed into a screen within a screen — the wake-up call

The "strategic brain" sits on the reader's side

Just waking up

You see through the present to find the next possibility

> *Overall....*

Motion "As-It-Is"

Power per stasis

Revoke the overall

Your eyes, not all by themselves

Subtext: Meta

Facial venting

Right where you are — through eternity

Grace punks up

Crisp multilayerings sharpen your senses

Mutually penetrating — inner elements & overtones radiating outward

Addressee unknown — "comparing and linking all points"

What's the "higher mathematics" of this fact, this movement

You'll leave the door unlocked

Force....

Bolshevatic hologram tattoo

Tenacity built-in

Subtext: scarecrow

In sequence: isn't this frame about to be shown being ignored, by an in-theater audience, who do get psyched up to watch something else?

Reciphering? Recoding?

So why define "attractions" as "shock moments"

'I must have been yelling at her. I must have scared her'

The "vanishing" becomes "irrevocable" — its force

Kinesthetic force impact

As some almost "communist decoding of the world"

Speed....

Pyro-

Subtext: fire

Slowness repatriated

Speed — of the modern (of *modernity*, the post-classical social body [or political economy] in which social change dubs itself Positive

Speed wakes you up — the aesthetic & the social

Speed coven

Frantic & then frozen — glacier-like — a tempo of the city

What if: accelerating out of control (anxiety attack-like heart rate)

Baring the device down to the wire — at the end of the spool, reduced to pure motion (even without substance: a spool turns empty)

Revolution....

Faktura — registers not only *movement*, but change

Communism in action

Change, fired up

The image projected to us by way of a screening-within-screen of a rotating (wire spool, film spool...)

The verb — to spin or rotate

Is this frame a secret 'dziga' rotation, a name based on a camera crank?

Preview: right before this frame — threads glow on a spinning loom, spinning wheel

Echo from the 'Editing Room' sequence — rotation of central spool, with filmstrip winding around it
Rotation anticipates shots of locomotive wheels (in a parallel composite) —

Revolution & Modernity; (& immediately after the locomotion: pictures of blockage & containment, class relations)

What's not up for grabs?

"a luchi nevidannykh dalëkikh mirov"
(but rays of invisible, distant worlds)

"luchi mertsaiushchikh zvëzd"
(rays of glimmering stars)

A remix of all these possibilities

A miniaturizing of utopian scale

Polyplausible

"impossible possibility"

Unless noted otherwise, everything in double quotation marks: Vertov's words

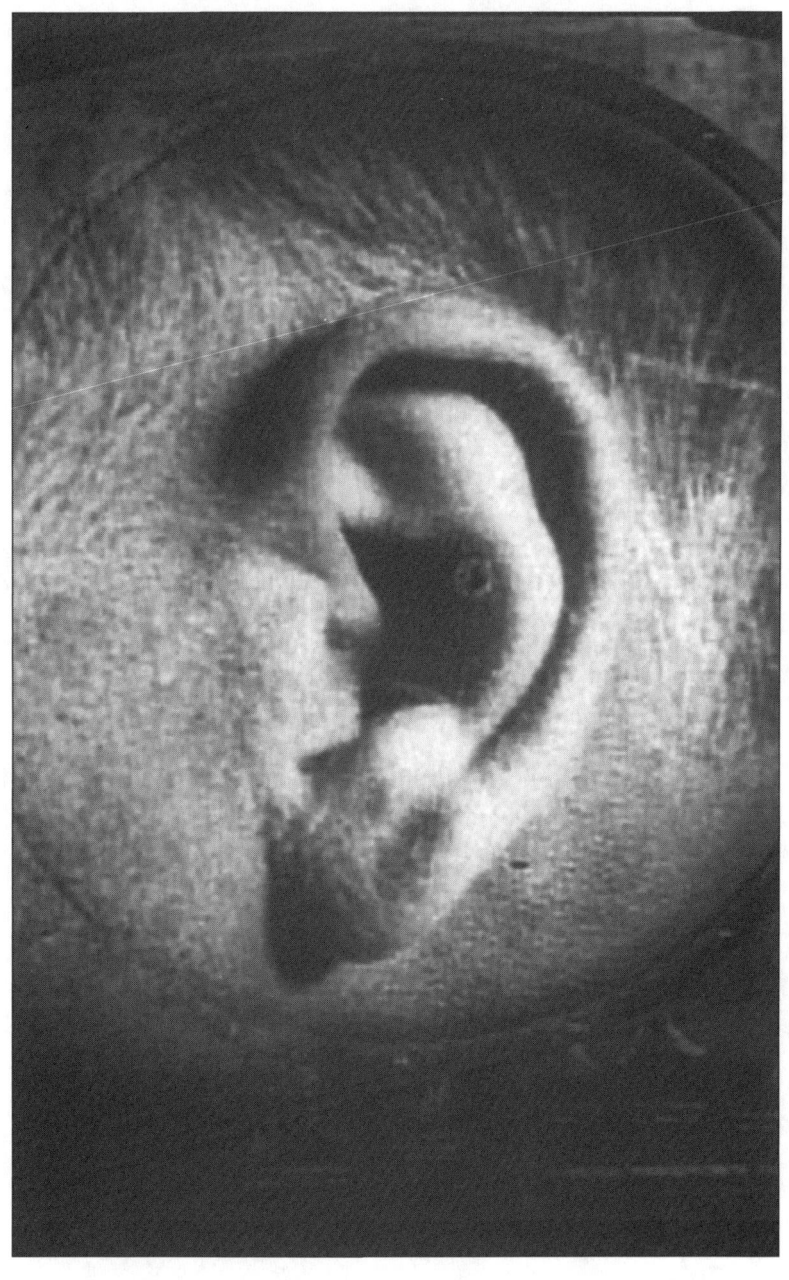

SOVIET DERVICHE

Abu Ali

> Explorar el caos de los fenomenos visuales que llenan el universo. Laboratorio del oído. Música de ruidos. Descubrir que el ojo puede registrar 2 o 3 fotogramas. Liberado de la estructura de tiempo y espacio coordino todos los puntos del universo, alli donde puedo registrarlos. Mi visión consiste en crear una nueva visión del mundo desconocida para vosotros y vosotras.

Dziga Vertov : Gira Peonza. Justo cruzar la frontera vuelvo a caer en un bloque blando de fiebre y sudores, psicodelia gratuita y un mensaje de mr zero: una imagen bobina, espiritu ululante, hilos de agua y acero torbellino. Probablemente Vertov fuese un derviche secreto de la hermandad sovietica: asamblearia y en sus manos otro pequeño girovago, el derviche mecanica cámara.

Tras la invocacion al oir los primeros notas de la flauta llorar el cañizal perdido, un derviche inicia el largo viaje circular rotando sobre un mismo punto, al girar son las cosas las que giran, es el mundo el que gira, probad sino el viejo truco de la infancia: parad en seco, el movimiento de las cosas no cesa, caemos aturdidos. El derviche alza una mano, desciende la otra, parece equilibrar para poder emborracharse mejor, mas profundamente, beber el vino, encontrarse él mismo en el contínuo de todas las cosas : la illaha ila allah: no hay mas realidad, que lo real y otros mantras secretos.

Gira, una y otra vez, mantiene el vértigo en ese caos que desfila ante él, ebrio en la sobriedad sobrio en la ebriedad, descubre primero que él está en realidad inmóvil es el universo el que gira a su alrededor, en el eje de una inmensa tormenta que lo eleva, podria incluso sentarse y tomar un café sin dejar de girar, pues ahora también las cosas que le orbitaban han desaparecido en el contínuo, especie de vapor de imágenes, liberado de la estructura espacio tiempo, una gota de agua en el oceáno.

SOVIET DERVISH

Abu Ali

> To explore the chaos of visual phenomena that fill the universe. Laboratory of hearing. Music of noise. To discover that the eye can register two or three frames. Freed from the structure of time and space, I coordinate all points in the universe, whereever I can register them. My vision consists of creating a new vision of the world unknown by you—either man or woman.

Dziga Vertov: Spinning Top. Precisely in crossing the frontier, I fall back into a soft block of fever and sweats, gratuitous psychedelia and a message from mrzero: an image that is a reel, howling spirit, threads of water and whirlwind of steel. Vertov was probably a secret dervish of the soviet brotherhood: it would assemble and in its hands another small wanderer: the mechanical camera dervish.

After the invocation, upon hearing the first notes of the flute crying out for the lost cane grove, a dervish initiates the long circular journey rotating upon a single point, when whirling, it is things that whirl, it is the world that whirls, just try the old childhood trick: stop dead, the movement of things doesn't cease, we fall back dazed. The dervish raises one hand, lowers the other, seems to balance in order to become more intoxicated, more deeply, to drink the wine, to find himself or herself in the continuum of all things: la illaha ila allah: there is no more reality, than the real and other secret mantras.

He whirls, again and again, maintains vertigo in this chaos that passes before him, drunk in sobriety, sober in drunkenness, discovers first that he is in reality immobile, it is the universe that whirls in his surroundings, in the axis of an immense storm that raises him up, he could even sit down and have a coffee without ceasing to whirl, since now it is the things that were orbiting around him which have disappeared in the continuum, a kind of vapor of images, liberated from space-time structure, a drop of water in the ocean.

Deberiamos ensayar las viejas visiones de Vertov bajo los mas viejos acordes de un taksim (x) o de un dikr: un recuerdo, un recuerdo de esa vision olvidada que anhelamos descubrir.

Un sadhu desnudo, cubierto con la blanca ceniza de los muertos realiza sus practicas, medita durante tres dias tumbado sobre un cadáver. Vertov lo hacia sobre los restos de metraje, las imágenes grabadas son siempre de muertos: instantes, objetos seres, tardes de verano desparecidas para siempre. Mapas del universo estrellas que ya no brillan.

El hombre con la cámara gira y gira riendo "la unidad nos libera, la libertad nos une".

We should test Vertov's old visions by means of the most ancient tones of a taksim or a dikr: a memory, a memory of this forgotten vision we wish to discover.

A naked sadhu, covered with the white ashes of the dead goes about his pratices, meditates for three days lying upon a cadaver. Vertov did the same on the remains of film footage—recorded images are always of the dead: instants, objects, beings, the summer afternoons which have disappeared forever. Maps of the universe, stars that no longer shine.

The man with the movie camera whirls and whirls laughing, "unity liberates us, liberty unites us."

FORWARD! BEFORE, DURING AND AFTER THE AUTHENTICALLY INTERNATIONAL ABSOLUTE LANGUAGE OF CINEMA, THE MOST IMPORTANT OF ALL THE ARTS

Ahwesh and Sanborn

THE RADICAL INDUSTRIALIZATION of the Soviet Union, including rural electrification, came about largely through Five Year Plans. When we proposed this project to its contributors, we did not intend for it to take so long to produce. In some respects we did better than the Soviets—we're taking only four years—though our ambitions were drastically lower, and our process entailed only one casualty: one of our contributors, in the time between his submission and today, defected to an academic press. *Vive l'anarchie.* Also in that interim, not only did Apple switch from Power PC to Intel processors, but *October* attempted to secure its long-standing territorial claim over matters Vertovian, not as against our claims—though they would no doubt dispute them—but as against the claims of at least one well-known theorist of so-called "new media."

Our interest in Vertov is at once personal and anecdotal and something more; let's call it sociological and historical. For artists who came of age in the late 1950s and 1960s, Vertov was the icon for what was once called "the radical aspiration" in film. It was while studying with and about that generation that we came to know Vertov's *Man with a Movie Camera*. It was also that iconic status that lead to the attempt to give the foundations of "new media" a Vertovian imprimatur. And that is understandable: *Man with a Movie Camera* is not only a radical unveiling of the means of cinematic production, it is the paradigm for what we might call *encyclopediac form*. It aims to give us an ambitious, complete, yet open view of a world, from A to Z, from production to post-production to projection to reception. And to create an opportunity for self-reflection in the viewer as the process of making a film unfolds *within* the film. Some of the greatest films of 1970s share parallel aspirations: *Zorn's Lemma, Rameau's Nephew…, La Société du spéctacle, Near the Big Chakra.*

It is not our aim here, however, to simply view Vertov through the wrong end of any particular historical or alphabetical telescope. Rather, our project is to try to understand just what Vertov might mean now, refracted through a muticiplicity of points of view. And in so doing, to better understand our own era. In order to do this, we focussed our attention on an image that we came to recognize as more or less indecipherable:

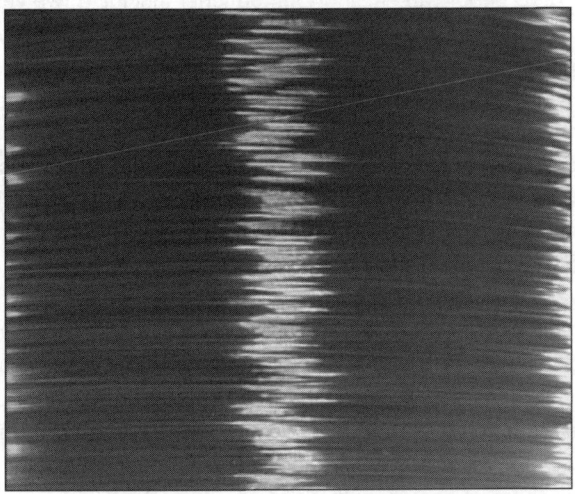

We chose this image as the result of conversations with friends over a period of several years about *Man with a Movie Camera*. We came to realize that while we could all agree on many aspects of the film—while differing in our interpretations—we could not help but notice, that the shot from which this image was taken opened up the greatest number of divergent speculations.

St. Augustine, in his *Confessions*, in speaking of miracles and textual exegesis, asserts that it is critical for the literal level of the text to be true. For him, this meant that before we proceed to the moral, anagogic, and eschatological aspects of a text, we must understand and, in the case of the bible, *believe* the literal meaning of the text. For us, then, what better way to unhinge the established certainties of meaning—in this film and in our world—than to start with an image of doubtful certainty, the interpretation of which is unlikely to produce consensus. We are interested in the act of interpretation on all levels: the creative misremembering and dismembering of the film through a digital translation of a single frame from a shot of dizzying instability.

That said, we did not intend this as a Rorschach test by which to trick people into publicly revealing their unconscious obsessions, though at least one person we solicited took it as such and refused to participate.

And so it was, that on September 22, 2003, we sent out to more than a hundred people an email or printed letter including two versions of the image in question (one large, one small) and a solicitation of their responses in whatever written form they chose. We promised them, in return for their labors, five copies of the printed book and the retention of their rights to their own contributions, except in the form of this anthology. We also guaranteed them that we would not edit their contributions. They would appear in the form in which they had been given to us in so far as it was possible.

We chose people we knew, people we admired from a distance, and people whom we thought might be interested. They were mostly theorists or artists; among the latter were painters, poets, filmmakers, video artists, "new media" artists, performance artists and those who promiscuously mingle all "disciplines." We asked them to write in one of eight European languages and offered to translate. We suggested responses from 250 to 10,000 words, though we made no absolute upper or lower limit. We asked them to let us know whether they would participate and set a deadline of January 1, 2004. We also asked for their discretion in not sharing their participation in the project with others without consulting us first.

We sent out reminders a few weeks later and again asked for those declining to participate to let us know, so no one would be left out accidentally. In the end, we received 40 responses of extraordinary quality and imagination. But for various reasons the project did not go forward to the printer. At last, one month shy of four years later, we are finalizing our layout and writing this "forward." We have not been able to offer, in the formula of the well-preserved comrade Lenin, Communism born of the power of the Soviets and the Electrification of the entire country, but we are certain that there is much in this anthology to incite reflections of an historical and a sociological nature in an era of global political dissarray and pervasive highspeed wireless traffic.

Our thanks go, first, to all the contributors. Of the many other people who helped with various aspects of this project, special thanks go to Su

Friedrich and Wendy Dougan for various forms of aid and assistance, to Rit Premnath for design suggestions, to Alain Cloarec and Catherine Ruéllo for help with translations, and to Diane Bertolo for expert critical review of our efforts at typesetting and book design, above and beyond the call. Last but not least, thanks should go to our patient and expert printer, McNaughton & Gunn.

Peggy Ahwesh and Keith Sanborn
Co-Authors of the Experiment
Assistants in Editing
October, 2007

CONTENTS

FORWARD! BEFORE, DURING AND AFTER THE AUTHENTICALLY INTERNATIONAL ABSOLUTE LANGUAGE OF CINEMA, THE MOST IMPORTANT OF ALL THE ARTS
Peggy Ahwesh & Keith Sanborn   160

SOVIET DERVISH
Abu Ali   156

CONSTRUCTIVISM MYSTERY
Bruce Andrews   134

Yann Beauvais   128

Ericka Beckman   127

EVERY MAN HIS OWN AURA
Walter Benjamin   126

Diane Bertolo   125

WORLD OF NAKED TRUTH
François Bucher   119

L'ORIGINE DU MONDE
Edwin Carels   115

FOUR LEGENDS FOR DZIGA
Abigail Child   111

VERTOV: BETWEEN TRANSPARENCY AND OPACITY
Ludovic Cortade   104

BRIAN FRYE 103

"VERTOV'S ACCIDENT' (OR, 'THE PAINT STILL')
JOY GARNETT 101

STOLEN
MARINA GRZINIC 100

VERTOV DIARIES 12/06/03-2/12/04
MICHELLE HANDELMAN 96

"I CAN'T SEE, VERTOV"
PETER HITCHCOCK 94

SPEED **MARX**
ROBERT KELLY 90

R&E&C&E&P&T&O&R&Y
MARINA DE BELLAGENTE LAPALMA 83

DAVID LARCHER 82

COUNTING INTERVAL IN FRACTIONAL DIMENSIONS
BARBARA LATTANZI 72

KINOEYE SEARCH
LES LEVEQUE 70

DISPATCH
DAVID LEVI STRAUSS 69

NEWS SUMMARY
Jeanne Liotta   67

THREE SONGS FOR VERTOV
Laura U. Marks   64

THE PICTURE
Julie Murray   60

SPOOL SPEECH
Kristin Prevallet   54

Cathy Nan Quinlan   53

ON THE GIGANTIC AND MINIATURE IN VERTOV'S MAN WITH A MOVIE CAMERA
Melissa Ragona   49

WIRELESS
John David Rhodes   47

WHILE AT THE KA DE CLUB
Jason Simon   44

SILENT FILM
John Smith   43

MY UNCLE BEN AND VERTOV
Michael Smith   41

HISTORY, THE COVENANT OF THE REMANT
ALAN SONDHEIM   37

A MODEST PROPOSAL VERTOV — RESPONSE
CASPAR STRACKE   34

tENTATIVELY A cONVENIENCE   30

LET IT BE THE MOON
BEATRIJS VAN AGT   26

THE FILM'S INDISSOLUBLE WHOLE?
MERCEDES VINCENTE   23

LOOKING FOR THE FILMIC IN A STILL FROM THE MAN WITH A MOVIE CAMERA
WILLIAM C. WEES   15

THE VERTOV IMAGE
PETER LAMBORN WILSON   14

DISINTEGRATION OF THE FRAME
GHEN ZANDO-DENNIS   6

THOMAS ZUMMER   3

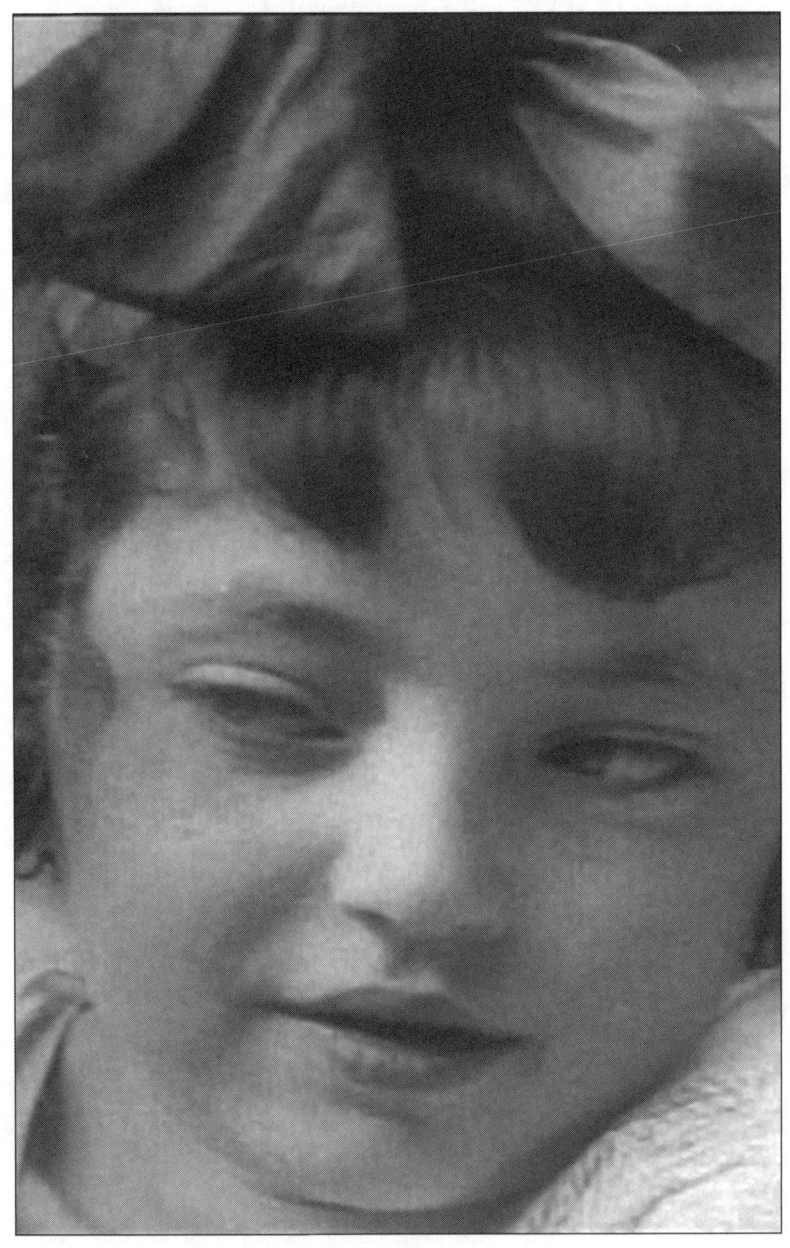